CORPUS PALLADIANUM

VOLUME VIII

CENTRO INTERNAZIONALE DI STUDI DI ARCHITETTURA
"ANDREA PALLADIO"

BOARD OF ADVISORS

CORPUS PALLADIANUM

Already published:

    I   THE ROTONDA, by Camillo Semenzato
   II THE BASILICA, by Franco Barbieri
  III THE CHIESA DEL REDENTORE, by Wladimir Timofiewitsch
  IV THE LOGGIA DEL CAPITANIATO, by Arnaldo Venditti
   V THE VILLA EMO AT FANZOLO, by Giampaolo Bordignon Favero
  VI THE CONVENTO DELLA CARITÀ, by Elena Bassi
 VII THE VILLA BADOER AT FRATTA POLESINE, by Lionello Puppi
VIII THE PALAZZO DA PORTO FESTA IN VICENZA, by Erik Forssman

In preparation:

THE PALAZZO ANTONINI IN UDINE, by Camillo Semenzato
THE PALAZZO CHIERICATI, by Franco Barbieri
THE PALAZZO THIENE IN VICENZA, by Renato Cevese
THE PALAZZO VALMARANA-BRAGA, by Nino Carboneri
THE VILLA BARBARO VOLPI AT MASER, by Giuseppe Mazzariol
THE VILLA CORNARO AT PIOMBINO DESE, by Douglas Lewis
THE VILLA MALCONTENTA AT MIRA, by Licisco Magagnato
THE VILLA PISANI AT BAGNOLO, by Marco Rosci
THE VILLA PISANI AT MONTAGNANA, by Carolyn Kolb Lewis and Francesco Cessi
THE VILLA SAREGO AT SANTA SOFIA DI PEDEMONTE, by Pietro Gazzola
THE TEATRO OLIMPICO, by Licisco Magagnato
THE UNREALIZED PROJECTS OF PALLADIO, by Manfredo Tafuri

Editor of the Series: Renato Cevese

Assistant Editor: Abelardo Cappelletti

THE PALAZZO DA PORTO FESTA

Erik Forssman

THE PALAZZO DA PORTO FESTA
IN VICENZA

CORPUS PALLADIANUM

VOLUME VIII

THE PENNSYLVANIA STATE UNIVERSITY PRESS

UNIVERSITY PARK & LONDON

The preparation of the monographs of the Corpus Palladianum has been made possible with the aid of the Consiglio Nazionale delle Ricerche of Italy and of the ENTI FONDATORI of the Centro Internazionale di Studi di Architettura "Andrea Palladio" in Vicenza.

I wish to thank my friend Renato Cevese for his unfailing assistance, without which this monograph would never have been written. For much useful and valuable information I thank Wolfgang Lotz and Rodolfo Pallucchini, both members of the Consiglio Scientifico, and Franco Barbieri, who is an inexhaustible mine of information on the monuments of Vicenza. Others who have aided me in various ways are Clemente di Thiene, Giangiacomo di Thiene, Manlio Sanmartin, and Robert Rowe. I am most grateful to Maria Costanza Festa Canera di Salasco for having allowed me free access to the palace, to the upkeep of which she has devoted herself diligently. And finally I wish to thank Maria Vittoria Pellizzari of the secretarial staff of the Center.

E. F.

Translated by Catherine Enggass

CONTENTS

Chapter I   The Patron

Chapter II   The Plans for Palazzo Porto

Chapter III   The Exterior and Interior of the Palace

Chapter IV   The Significance of Palazzo Porto in the Work
of Palladio and in the History of Architecture

Chapter V   The Surviving Interior Decorations of the Sixteenth
and Eighteenth Centuries

Bibliography

Index of Names and Places

List of Illustrations in the Text

List of Plates

List of Scale Drawings

NOTE

Illustrations in the text are cited with the prefix "fig." and a Roman numeral. Plates are cited with the prefix "fig." and an Arabic numeral.

THE PALAZZO DA PORTO FESTA

I

THE PATRON

The Porto family appears in Vicenza about the eleventh century. From that time on, many members of the family played important roles in the history of Vicenza and the Venetian Republic. By the beginning of the eighteenth century the distinguished family had been subdivided into ten branches, so that it is often very hard to determine to which branch individual members of the family belonged.[1] The Porto family received the title of count from Charles V in 1532 when the emperor passed through the Veneto on his way to Bologna. From that date, the two-headed imperial eagle and the crown appear in their coat-of-arms.[2] In the sixteenth century Ippolito da Porto especially distinguished himself by conquering the Protestants at Mühlberg; he was later named commander of the Venetian forces on Corfù.

Da Schio calls the man who gave the commission for the palace "one of the gentlemen who was most active in promoting the glory of his country and of Palladio in the sixteenth century."[3] We do not know the basis of this assertion since the known documents concerning Iseppo da Porto are few.[4] We do know that he was the son of a Gerolamo da Porto, who owned a palace in Contrà Porti, as did many members of his family, but the date of his birth is unknown. A portrait in the Villa Colleoni-Thiene at Thiene (fig. IV) bears the inscription "IOSEPHUS PORTUS. ANNO DOMINI MDLII. AETATIS VERO SUAE XXXII," but its authenticity is still to be verified. He married Livia Thiene in the early 1540s.[5] In fact, in 1539 when that famous theatrical representation for which Sebastiano Serlio executed the scenery was held "in the great Porto courtyard"[6] (the courtyard of the Porto-Colleoni palace, next door to Palladio's palace), Lucrezio Beccanuvoli mentions Livia Thiene in a poem about the ladies present at the spectacle. From this we know that she was not yet married in 1539.[7] We know also that from 1542 Livia's brother, Marco Antonio, was in contact with Palladio regarding the project for Palazzo Thiene.[8]

The marriage of Iseppo da Porto and Livia Thiene was blessed by the birth of five girls and two boys. In a portrait by Paolo Veronese (fig. II) we see Iseppo with his elder son Adriano, who must have been about seven at the time; another portrait (fig. III) shows Livia da Porto with her daughter Porzia, who was perhaps two years younger than her brother. If it is true that the marriage took place between 1542 and 1545 we can date the two portraits to about 1553. In the portrait Iseppo da Porto appears to be a man of about thirty-five. His face is stern. We do not know whether he had any intellectual interests; however, it is certain that the portrait does not show a particularly lively expression. In a medal that is attributed to Alessandro Vittoria,[9] inscribed "IOSEPHUS PORTIUS COMES VICENTIE," his face does not have a well-defined character, only a certain sense of pride. If the medal is to be dated in the years 1552-53, when Vittoria was in Vicenza working for Iseppo's brother-in-law in Palazzo Thiene, then it would be contemporary with the portrait. But since Iseppo appears in profile in the medal and in full face in the portrait it is difficult to compare them. He was at one time (after 1556) made *principe* of the Accademia Olimpica, but we do not know if he carried out any significant action during his tenure in that office.[10] His elder son Adriano married Anna Malaspina and in a genealogical tree of the seventeenth century is described "Vir humanissimus et summa probitate decoratus," but no reasons are given for such praise.[11] About Leonida we know only that he celebrated his marriage to Attilia Thiene in 1570. Four of Iseppo's daughters married Vicentine noblemen, and Deidamia, probably the youngest, entered a convent.

It is possible that at the time of his wedding Iseppo had already acquired the land for his palace; and it would be understandable for him to have preferred land in Contrà Porti, where so many of his relatives lived. But it was no easy task for the architect to utilizie the narrow space between Contrà Porti and Strada degli Stalli for a town house of some pretensions (scale drawing I).

The date when the work was begun cannot be precisely established. Temanza says that he read the date "1552" on the palace,[12] but the inscription was obliterated during the nineteenth century restoration. Allowing that Iseppo da Porto thought of building his palace soon after his marriage, that is, in the years 1542-45,

then Palladio's plans for Palazzo Thiene and Palazzo Porto Festa would have been contemporary, that is during the first half of the 1540s, certainly not 1551.

Iseppo da Porto also had a villa at Molina between Marano and Thiene. Two long colonnaded *barchesse* or farm buildings (probably of a later date), very rustic in appearance with ten more or less fragmentary columns made for a portico or a colonnade that was never finished, still remain.[13] On the base of a column Zorzi read the name "Iosephus" and the date 1572. Earlier, Magrini had noted and attributed to Palladio this Villa Porto-Colleoni (now Thiene) in Molina[14] It is in fact very likely that Iseppo would have wanted the same architect to whom he had entrusted the contruction of this city residence for his country residence as well. Unfortunately it is impossible to reconstruct Palladio's plan from the little that now remains of what was built. From the dimensions of the columns we can assume that the villa had been designed on a very large scale, almost like that which the Villa Thiene at Quinto would have acquired, judging from the illustrations of the *Secondo Libro* of the *Trattato*.

On 5 December 1570, probably shortly before his death, Iseppo made his will.[15] He was buried in the church of S. Biagio, which is near Palazzo Porto, and beside him rests his wife Livia. The church was deconsecrated in 1810 and during the nineteenth century it was turned into a military depot. Today it is a garage.[16] No trace remains in the building of the ancient and splendid monuments: the tomb of Iseppo and Livia Porto no longer exists. Their son Adriano had a commemorative tablet made for his parents, whose inscription, as reported by Faccioli, read: "IOSEPHO PORTIO PATRI EQ. CLARISS. AC LIVIAE THIENAE MATRI OPT. VIV. SIBI AC POSTERIS ADRIANUS FILIUS. HSPC OBIIT ANNO MDLXXX

I - Alessandro Vittoria (?), *Medal with the portrait of Iseppo da Porto (recto and verso)*

II - Paolo Veronese, *Portrait of Iseppo da Porto with his son Adriano*. Florence, Uffizi

III - PAOLO VERONESE, *Portrait of Livia da Porto with daughter*. Baltimore, Walters Art Gallery

IV - Unknown Venetian Painter of the Sixteenth Century, *Portrait of Iseppo da Porto*.
Thiene, Villa da Porto, now Thiene

V - ANDREA PALLADIO, *First design for the façade of Palazzo da Porto Festa*. London, R.I.B.A., XVII, 12r

DIE VIII NOV." [17] The funeral monument was placed in front of the altar that Adriano had donated in 1594 and which was adorned with a painting by Alessandro Maganza.

In his will Iseppo made his two sons his sole heirs, but he favored Adriano with the addition of 5000 ducats. He ensured to his wife a life interest in all his possessions. When the division of his estate took place on 21 July 1581 Leonida drew by lot Palazzo Porto, while the villa in Molina was divided between the brothers. An appraisal of the estate was made by Giandomenico Scamozzi. [18]

Adriano, who made his will in 1605 in favor of his relatives, died without direct heirs. Leonida, the younger son, had two sons and grandsons and thus the palace remained in the possession of the Porto family up to the beginning of the present century. The last of the Porto proprietors were Gentile Colleoni-Porto, who held the palace until 1860, and Guardino Colleoni-Porto, who sold it to Count Luigi Biego on 12 December 1907. On 6 October 1920 the Lanificio Rossi Company of Milan acquired the palace and subsequently sold it on 10 November 1928 to the Angelo Festa e Figlio Company of Vicenza. Since 1945 the palace has belonged to Italo Festa, and, after his death, to his wife Maria Costanza dei Conti Canera di Salasco. [19] The present proprietor has dedicated herself with devotion to the conservation and restoration of the palace, as her husband did before her.

VI - Andrea Palladio, *Second design for the façade of Palazzo da Porto Festa*. London, r.i.b.a., XVII, 9r

NOTES TO CHAPTER I

Works cited in the notes only by the author's surname and date may be found fully described under that date in the Bibliography.

[1] The oldest and most complete genealogical tree seems to be in the *Istoria Genealogica della famiglia Porto Nobile Vicentina scritta da Francesco Tomasini MDCC*, a manuscript in the Bertoliana Library of Vicenza. In it is cited a document of 1082 by which the Emperor Henry IV confirmed the ownership of a property by the jurisconsul Porto, who is cited without a first name and identified only as from Vicenza.

[2] In this regard see Rumor, 1887, pp. 29 ff.

[3] Da Schio, *Memorabili*, vol. Pas-Pu, manuscript in the Bertoliana Library of Vicenza. There are in it many erroneous statements about the patron of the palace. It is odd that Iseppo da Porto was not mentioned by G. Marzari in his work of 1591. All the Vicentine nobles worthy of mention appear in this work. Marzari does not even cite the sons of Iseppo.

[4] The little that we can report here is taken from the Colleoni-Porto archives in the villa-castle of Thiene, to which, through the kindness of Count Clemente di Thiene, I was given access. The archives are in perfect order, but unfortunately I was able to find little information concerning the patron. The archival documents on the genealogy of the Porto family in the Bertoliana Library are being catalogued and were not available to me. When

these documents can be consulted the chronology of the palace, here sketched out, may be clarified.

[5] The year 1545 was suggested by Pallucchini, 1939, and repeated by Piovene and Marini, 1968, where on p. 92 we read: "Archival research carried out by G. Fasolo confirms that Count Giuseppe da Porto married Lucia Thiene in 1545, and that of the seven children born of the marriage the first was called Adriano and the second Porzia." Fasolo's archival studies unfortunately have been ignored by Veronese scholars.

In the index of the Porto-Godi-Pigafetta papers in the Bertoliana Library of Vicenza there is a document catalogued under the number 1094, dated "Ult. Febb. 1542," according to which Giovanni Galeazzo Thiene arranged a dowry of 4000 ducats for his daughter Livia when she was affianced to Iseppo da Porto. Therefore the marriage must have taken place a short time later, perhaps even that same year.

[6] The description of the theater in Serlio, 1545, bk. II. See also Magagnato, 1954, p. 40.

[7] *Tutte le Donne vicentine, matitate, Vedove e Dongelle per Lucrezio Beccanuvoli Bolognese* (1539). In the introduction the year 1539 is cited and there one reads: "The most splendid play held on the Sunday of Carnival at the request of the very illustrious gentlemen of the Calza Vicentini was given in the great court of the Porto family."

8 Scholars are not yet in agreement about when the project for Palazzo Thiene was conceived. CEVESE, 1952, p. 52, first called attention to the 1542 contract, according to which Marc' Antonio Thiene entered into an agreement, which Palladio witnessed, with two masons for the construction of a palace. Cevese correctly stated: "The presence of the illustrious architect constitutes evidence whose importance cannot be disregarded." Further clarification may be expected from a later volume of the Corpus Palladianum.

9 Concerning the medal, which today, in the original and in a die of the nineteenth century, is in the Civic Museum of Vicenza, see MORSOLIN, 1892, V. fasc. III. CESSI, 1960, makes no mention of the medal for Iseppo da Porto.

10 ZORZI, 1968, p. 261, in which in a document "Olympici Principes ab anno MDLVI ad annum MDCVII," we find the name "Iosephus Portius."

11 The geneaological tree is found in the Colleoni-Porto archives in Thiene, mazzo XL, n. 636.

12 TEMANZA, 1762, p. VIII.

13 On Villa Molina near Thiene see ZORZI, 1968, pp. 228 ff.

14 MAGRINI, 1845, p. 294.

15 A copy of the testament is in the Colleoni-Porto archives in Thiene, mazzo LI, n. 708.

16 On the church of S. Biagio, see RUMOR, *Guida*, MS vol. 6, in the Bertoliana Library of Vicenza.

17 FACCIOLI, 1776, vol. I, p. 205. The date on the tombstone (8 November 1580) contradicts the date of the testament (5 December 1580), a problem that cannot now be clarified.

18 The division of the goods is dated 21-7-1581 and is found in the Colleoni-Thiene archives, mazzo LI, n. 720.

19 The will of Adriano is cited in the *Istoria Genealogica* (see note 1 above). For the information about the owners in the late nineteenth and twentieth century I am indebted to dott. Manlio Sanmartin for this research, which he generously allowed me to consult.

II

THE PLANS FOR PALAZZO PORTO

The stages in the planning of Palazzo Porto can be reconstructed from five drawings in the collection of the Royal Institute of British Architects in London.[1] There are three for the façade and two for the ground plan. The first scheme (fig. V) for the façade (R.I.B.A. XVII, 12r) has remarkable similarities with Casa Civena, which is dated 1540. The *piano nobile* is divided by Corinthian pilasters and has seven windows capped by small pediments that are alternately triangular and curvilinear. The windows, surrounded by plain frames without moldings or corbeled volutes, rest on a simple socle. The unbroken wall extends up over the windows, with rather unhappy results. The ground-floor façade was rusticated, and Palladio must have planned to have strongly projecting blocks, as we see in the drawing where the rustication is worked out in greater detail on the left side of a window and the right side of the arched portal. To the left of the portal one can make out two columns, which carry a segment of entablature and the impost of an arch. Here Palladio apparently wished to introduce the Serlian motif as a central element. The Serlian motif also appears in a pair of drawings for palace façades that were probably designed shortly after Palladio's first trip to Rome. In these drawings the Serlian motif appears not on the ground level at the entrance portal but on the upper story.[2] The first drawing, moreover, gives two variants for the ground-floor façade of Palazzo Porto. On the left side there is a smooth continuous base under the windows; on the right side the entire wall is rusticated.

For the dating of this drawing one must take into account its closeness in conception and in graphic execution to designs of palaces and villas, for the most part unexecuted, that can be dated around 1540-45.[3] It clearly reveals a knowledge of the Casa di Raffaello of Bramante,[4] as well as the palaces by Sanmicheli in Verona, and it is possible to find also a hint, at least in the ground floor, of Falconetto's dryest manner. The superimposition of a high *piano nobile* of the Corinthian order upon a rusticated basement story also appears in Palazzo Thiene, which was designed in 1542 or a little later. In Palazzo Thiene, however, the details became richer and more plastic in the course of execution. Thus, it seems logical to date the first plan for the façade of Palazzo Porto around 1542. As we have seen, Palladio was working for the Thiene family from 1542 and, presumably, the marriage between Livia Thiene and Iseppo da Porto took place in that same year. On such an occasion it would be completely natural that there be discussion about a residence suitable for a person of Iseppo da Porto's rank.

VII - ANDREA PALLADIO, *Third design for the façade of Palazzo da Porto Festa.* London, R.I.B.A., XVII, 12v

Probably a little later Palladio executed in a single drawing (R.I.B.A. XVII, 9 r) two more variants for the façade of Palazzo Porto (fig. VI). On the right the Corinthian pilasters are retained, but the windows are more richly contoured and ornamented with corbeled volutes, according to the rules of Vitruvius. It includes another story with rectangular windows broader than they are high, creating the effect of a giant order, as in Sanmicheli's Palazzo Canosso. The base is scarcely varied, but the proportions of the windows are conceived more harmoniously.[5]

In the variant on the left, the ground-floor windows, which rest on smooth bases, are more richly enframed with moldings and corbeled volutes. Tondi are lightly sketched in above the windows, very likely for the placement of busts, as in the case of the Casa Civena. But Palladio eliminated decoration that lacked monumentality and substituted rustication. The variation on the left provides a remarkable innovation through the rearrangement of the *piano nobile.* Here we find a true Ionic order of engaged columns appearing for the first time in Palladio's work.

In this variation the tendency toward the flattening of the reliefs, a characteristic of Palladio's youthful designs, seems to have been overcome. Indeed, with this plan, Palladio approached the plasticity characteristic of the façade executed in his maturity. Moreover, the separation of the top story from the *piano nobile* is new and important. The resolution of the top story into an attic makes the articulation of the façade into three stories stand out clearly.

Bramante had disguised the top story of the Casa di Raffaello through the decoration of the *piano nobile* by opening small windows between the triglyphs of the Doric order. The only building that Palladio presumably took into account for his new design was Raphael's Palazzo Caffarelli in Rome, where the third story has in fact become an attic. Such a superimposition of three stories, made up of a ground floor, *piano nobile*, and attic, was of great importance not only for Palladio but for all civil architecture of the following two centuries.

A third plan (fig. VII) for the façade (R.I.B.A. XVII, 12 v) shows only the ground floor, and this in two variants. The variant on the right differs little from the first drawing, the Serlian motif that functions as a portal returning once again, while the variant on the left anticipates the façade as it was actually executed, in that the five stones embedded above the windows are set within an arch with shallow, smooth-surfaced lunettes.

If we consider the three plans together we see how, the nearer he comes to the definitive design, the more Palladio proceeds graphically toward a more plastic form. All of these drawings are, like his youthful works, free of decorations in relief and statues. They are limited to strictly architectonic forms and are marked by that type of Roman severity to which he returns only in Palazzo Thiene. The final plan, that is, the one that was the working basis for the present façade of Palazzo Porto is missing. The engraving in the *Secondo Libro* cannot substitute for it; rather, it is a later reworking of what was actually built. The same holds true, as we will see later, in regard to the ground plan.

Only two designs can with absolute certainty be considered preparatory studies for the ground plan of Palazzo Porto,

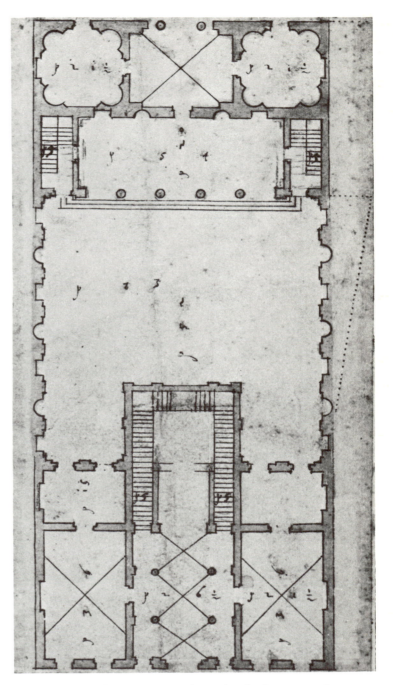

VIII - Andrea Palladio, *First design for the floor plan of Palazzo da Porto Festa.* London, R.I.B.A., XVI, 8

since their scale corresponds to the area and to the form of the executed building. The first ground plan is certainly the one reproduced here as fig. VIII; according to it the palace is entered through a gallery 36 by 26.5 feet, whose groin vault is supported by four columns. Two large rooms, 36 by 21.5 feet, open at each side. These lead into two smaller rooms, 21.5 by 15 feet, the windows of which look into the courtyard. As we see, these spaces do not relate to one another by simple proportions. At the end of the gallery there is a monumental stairwell, which on the ground level also serves as the passageway between the atrium and the courtyard. Two flights of stairs at right angles to each other lead to the *piano nobile*. The distribution of the rooms there would probably have had to correspond to that of the ground floor, that is, above the gallery there would have to be the salon, and above the stairs an entrance hall. The courtyard is square and does not have a colonnade. The lateral walls have niches that are alternately semicircular and square, a motif that Palladio had seen, for example, in Villa Madama. At the end of the court there is a loggia of five intercolumniations, that perhaps, like the Cornaro loggia at Padua, would have served also as a theater stage. But at the same time it is the façade of a two-story house, which also has an entrance with an atrium on Strada degli Stalli. On the two sides of this atrium there are octagonal rooms with semicircular niches. In the Odeo Cornaro we also find an octagonal room that served as a salon, and Palladio himself introduced it in the corner rooms of Palazzo Thiene.

Of special importance in this first design for the ground plan of Palazzo Porto is the stairwell. For half the distance it is freestanding and on three sides it faces the court. The union of the stairs and the entry to the court is completely new. This element in the center of the house thus serves for both horizontal and vertical communication. Palladio, however, was not in a position to realize this concept in his buildings. Only in the palaces of the Baroque period will the stairway take on the role of the central nucleus. Alberti considered the stairway as an inescapable obstacle: "The less stairs there are in a

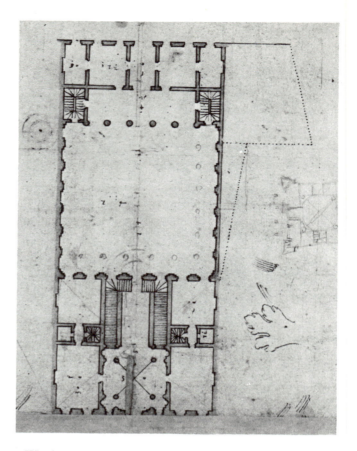

IX - ANDREA PALLADIO, *Second design for the floor plan of Palazzo da Porto Festa*. London, R.I.B.A., XVII, 9v

building and the less space they take, the more convenient will the building be." [6] Palladio, on the other hand, derived from them an essential element for order and movement in space. He stated: "The stairs will be successful if they are bright, spacious, and convenient to climb: whence they almost invite people to ascend... They will be sufficiently spacious if they do not appear narrow and cramped in relation to the size and quality of the building." [7]

The stairway must therefore be in a close relationship with the magnificence of the entire building, since it is part of its "decorum." Palladio never applied that concept as thoroughly as he did in the first floor plan for Palazzo Porto. In the second floor plan (R.I.B.A. XVII, 9 v) he reduced somewhat the monumentality of the stairway (fig. IX), since it is enclosed in the body of the house. For that reason it receives less light. The transformation was necessary because the gallery has now become a tetrastyle atrium. Later, adhering to the theories of Vitruvius, Palladio described it in the *Secondo Libro*, where he said: "From the atrium one passes through the tablinum into the peristyle." The narrow passage between the stairs could be interpreted as the tablinum. The uncolonnaded court has pilasters on three sides that could well take the place of columns, while on the fourth side, as in the first project, there is a portico that constitutes the entrance to the house in back. The rooms of this building were simplified with respect to the first plan, probably for practical reasons.

In the main section the rooms are changed in accordance with simple harmonic proportions. Apart from the square rooms, the proportion is now 3 : 2, that is to say, the two large rooms on either side of the atrium measure 30 by 20 feet. Also new are the two small unlighted stairways reserved for service functions. Comparing this plan with that of the *Secondo Libro*, it is obvious that there is a general correspondence. In fact only the double stairway has disappeared, and a single stairway has been put in its place.

Palladio must have devoted much time to the development of the ground plan and the façade. The shape of the area between the two streets made it necessary to turn to the Venetian tradition. The palaces of the city on the lagoons are compressed between a canal in front and a narrow street in back. While the Florentine palaces occupy an entire block and have arcaded courts on four sides, the Venetian courts have a colonnade only on one side or none at all. This traditional element Palladio made his own in the first designs for Palazzo Porto. The four main walls that constitute the fundamental

structure of the building, continuous and parallel to one another, also derive from the Venetian tradition and have no similarity with Roman and Florentine palaces. In the Venetian palace the central axis is constituted by the *portego* (portico), which is developed through the whole depth of the house. In the two designs we might be able to recognize the motif of the *portego* even if in a changed form.

Some particular aspects of the first plan for the back area of the house come from the architecture of Falconetto. In the elevation, however, they disappear behind the great colonnade. While the first design still relates to the Venetian and Paduan tradition, the second one reveals an attempt to blend that tradition with the structure of the ancient Roman house as it was described by Vitruvius and derived from him by Palladio.[8] In the court that earlier had been conceived without columns, columns were later added in pencil, changing it into a regular peristyle. Thus emerges the succession of atrium, tablinum, and peristyle, characteristics of the Vitruvian house. If, moreover, one adds to this the fact that the façade shows the influence of the Roman architecture of Bramante and Raphael and also of the palaces of Sanmicheli, one may conclude that classical antiquity, Rome, Venice, Padua, and Verona are present in the designs of Palazzo Porto. Studying the palace in its actual form we will try to explain how a typically Palladian work could come from these diverse components.

Between the second plan and the start of construction another design was probably made in which the double stairway was eliminated and in its place were substituted two rooms of slight importance. The existence of such a design may be deduced from the first description of Palazzo Porto made by Palladio, that is, not from the *Secondo Libro* but from a manuscript in the Correr Museum. It was written before 1565 and shows the palace as the artist initially conceived it and as it was in the course of construction at that date. "The ground plan and the elevation shown below are of the house of Count Iseppo de Porti in Vicenza. The entrances have four columns of the Doric order fifteen feet in height, and at the sides two rooms half again as long as wide. The height of the vaults is in accordance with harmonic proportions. From these rooms one passes through corridors into other square rooms to which are joined two small rooms, the vaults of which are thirteen feet high. Several of these rooms have very charming decorations with beautiful paintings by Brusasorzi of Verona and marvelous stuccoes by Ridolfi. By means of the corridors opposite the entranceways one enters a loggia that goes around the whole courtyard. Its columns are thirty-six and one-half feet high, and behind them are pilasters that support the floor of the second loggia. These lofty columns, along with the architrave, frieze, and cornice, reach to the level of the floor of the attic and create an open platform like small terraces; above each one a statue is to be placed. The size of the salon is indicated by the large axis: the length is the diagonal of the square times the width and it is as high as it is wide and has two orders of windows. In the back part one finds something like another house, that is to say, kitchens and women's quarters. I have placed the large stairway that corresponds to half the court so that it may be convenient to both parts and so that those who want to go up above would have to see the most beautiful parts of the house. The cellars and other like places are underground. The stables lie outside the area of the engraving."[9]

From this description it seems that the floor plan of the house had very nearly

arrived at the form it takes in the *Secondo Libro*. Data concerning the salon on the *piano nobile* are very interesting: the relationship between the width and length is 1 : 2. The salon faced Contrà Porti on the short side, while an antechamber faced the court. After the nineteenth century restoration nothing remained of this area. The description of the back house is also very important inasmuch as it does not seem to be laid out as a simple doubling of the house proper, but as "another house" that contained "kitchens and women's quarters." It is probable that such an arrangement comes from the description of the Greek house made by Vitruvius in the *Sesto Libro*, chapter 7. According to that description, the Greeks were inclined to build the rooms of the women, "the gynaeceum," on the side of the peristyle opposite the entrance. Palladio provided no specifications for the ground plan of this house. Nevertheless, we may imagine that what he had in mind was something like the second plan. The communication between the main house and the women's house must have been by means of the peristyle.

On one side of the peristyle the great stairway, which we see later in the floor plan of the *Secondo Libro* (fig. XI), had already been envisaged. Compared to the great double stairway in the drawings, it appears without doubt to be a later solution and certainly a less successful one. Neither the one set nor the other was built, but the patron surely could not have been satisfied with two narrow and dark spiral stairways provided for the servants. According to Muttoni there had been a stairway on the right, which began "immediately at the entrance and had fourteen steps running in a straight line, about five feet wide," and then "continued with another thirty steps arranged in an oval, with a column in the middle going down

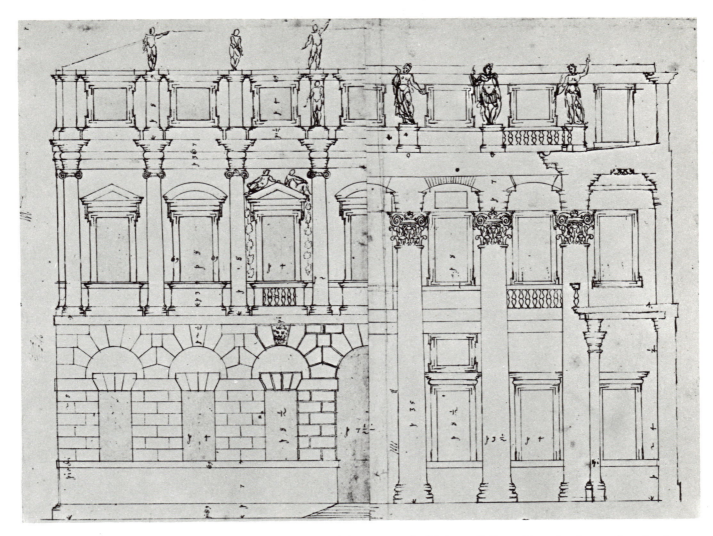

X - ANDREA PALLADIO, *Design of the front elevation and the courtyard of Palazzo da Porto Festa for the woodcut for the*
Quattro Libri. London, R.I.B.A., XVII, 3

to the floor," which served "as the entrance to the salon." Muttoni thought it was "very likely, though not certain, that such a correction, rather than change, had been made by Palladio himself." [10]

Around 1560 Palladio designed oval stairs for several buildings, including the Convento della Carità in Venice and the Villa Sarego at S. Sofia near Verona. It is likely, therefore, that he made a further variation in the design of Palazzo Porto after deciding not to build the peristyle and the great stairway. In the nineteenth-century renovation both the spiral stairs at the left of the entrance and the oval stairs at the right disappeared.

When Palladio finished the text and drawings for the definitive edition of the *Secondo Libro*, after 1565, nothing of the peristyle or the house in back had been built. For years the main house had been finished and lived in, but there was probably no more than discussion about enlarging it by the addition of a court and a rear block. There was certainly the intention of building the women's quarters in accordance with the Greek manner until, being counter to every local tradition, the project was finally abandoned. Moreover, Palladio of course knew that the Greeks housed not just the women but also the guests in separate buildings. Therefore, in the *Secondo Libro* when he designed the Greek house according to the dictates of Vitruvius, the guest quarters in his reconstruction were self-contained blocks placed along the sides of the peristyle: "Close to this building there will be on the left and right other houses that have their own individual doors, and all the conveniences for living therein, and in those houses will reside the guests, who will be free in all respects as if they were in their own home." [11]

Since the land available for Palazzo Porto did not permit lateral guest quarters, it was obvious that the back house toward Strada degli Stalli was utilized for that purpose. But Palladio, instead of drawing up a new ground plan for the guest quarters, was content to repeat the plan of the main house in back of the peristyle. This way of proceeding was not correct according to Vitruvius, nor did it reflect the idea of the Greek house that he himself had proposed. As we have seen, the main house with its atrium, tablinum, and peristyle was inspired by the principles of the house of the ancient Romans. In such a context, the insertion of elements characteristic of the Greek house is not very logical. Therefore the view commonly held that the plan of Palazzo Porto in the *Secondo Libro* (fig. XI) expresses the original idea of Palladio is erroneous. It was, on the contrary, a way of resolving *a posteriori* the incongruity between the idea and the reality, and took form only in the engraving in the *Secondo Libro*. The plan, moreover, shows little imagination: the duplication of the main house would have led to an abstract and uniform monumentality, something that, in practice, we never encounter in Palladio's work. The caption dealing with Palazzo Porto, as it appears in the *Secondo Libro*, was entirely rewritten by Palladio a little before 1570, certainly as a comment on the doubled ground plan. At the same time the artist introduced some notable observations about the part of the palace already constructed: "The designs that fol-low are of the house of Count Iseppo de' Porti, a most noble family of the above-named city. This house faces two public streets, thus having two entrances, each of which has four columns that support the vault and make the area above safe. The ground-floor rooms are vaulted. The height of these rooms, which are adjacent to the aforesaid entrances, is in accordance with the last mode for the height of vaults. The secondary rooms, that is, those on the upper floor, have flat ceilings. The grounds floor rooms, like those rooms above, in that part of the building that has been built, are decorated with paintings and with very beautiful stuccoes by the hands of the above-named skillful men and by Messer Paolo Veronese, most excellent painter. The court is surrounded by colonnades that go from the aforesaid entrances by means of a gallery. They will have columns of thirty-six and one-half feet in height, that is to say, as high as the first and second order. Behind these columns are pilasters one and three-quarters feet wide and one foot and two inches thick, which will support the floor of the loggia above. The court divides the whole house into two parts: that part in front will serve for the use of the owner and his women; that in back will be for the housing of guests: whereby the household members and the guests will remain free in every respect; something that the ancients and especially the Greeks held in high regard. Moreover, this partition would serve in the event the descendants of the aforesaid gentleman would want to have separate apartments. I wanted to place the principal stairs under the colonnade that corresponds to the middle of the court in order that those who wish to climb above would be compelled to view the most beautiful part of the building; and also, so that it might serve both parts, it is in the middle. The cellars and similar

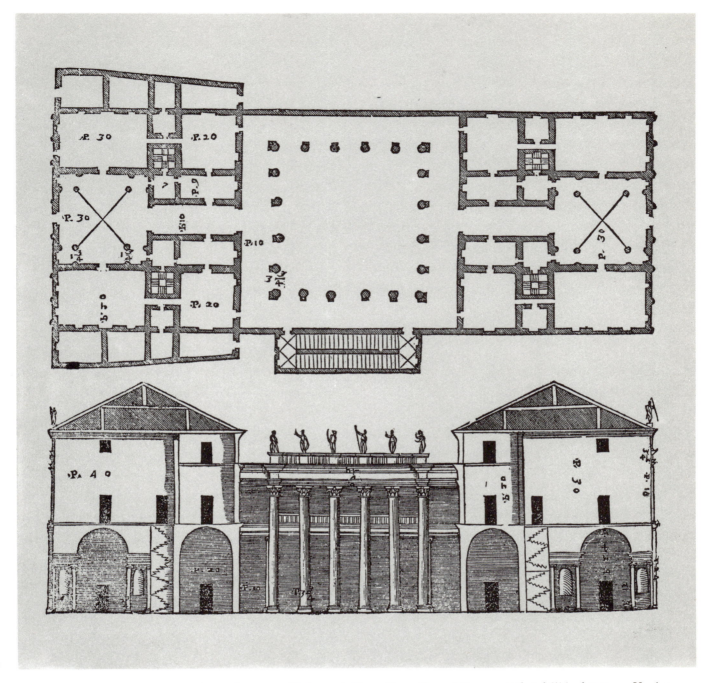

XI - ANDREA PALLADIO, *Floor plan and section of Palazzo da Porto Festa*. From *I Quattro Libri dell'Architettura*, Venice, 1570, II, chapter III, p. 8

areas are underground. The stables are outside the body of the house: and the entrance to them is under the stairs. The first of the large drawings is of the façade, and the second is of the court."

In contrast to the first draft of the text (Correr Museum Ms) it is here stated that the women also live in the main house. And the duplication of the building is still motivated by the affirmation that not only the guests but also the descendants of the owner of the house — principally the two sons, Adriano and Leonida — would have separate apartments.

Considering the design for the façade, it is clear that it would have had a rich plastic decoration. Only the ground floor corresponds to the actual building. While in the elevation in the *Secondo Libro* all the windows are decorated with reclining figures of a Michelangelesque flavor and with festoons, in the design as realized only the central window and the two at either end have this kind of decoration. In the elevation the statues are freestanding above the attic, providing an imaginative termination of the entire project. In the realization, on the other hand, they have been placed on the cornice of the Ionic order in front of the pilasters of the attic, and there are only four instead of eight. Palladio had envisaged allegorical female figures, while the four existing statues represent members of the Porto family. One may then conclude that the decoration of the windows of the *piano nobile* existed before 1570, but that the statues of the attic probably were put in place after the publication of the *Secondo Libro* in 1570.

The façade facing Strada degli Stalli would have been further extended by two intercolumniations in comparison with the façade on Contra' Porti according to the plan in the *Secondo Libro*. Since it also faces on Piazza di S. Biagio, it would have become the principal façade of the palace. It is logical to think that it would have been decorated in a way similar to the façade that was built. From the plan it is not possible to deduce how the lateral parts would have been resolved. The problem is not of great importance, since after the appearance of the *Secondo Libro* the duplication toward Strada degli Stalli was no longer under serious consideration.

In the R.I.B.A. collection (XVII, 3) there is also a sixth drawing (fig. X) that has been considered as the "definitive plan of the palace, in part carried out."[12] But such an interpretation is erroneous, since we are dealing with a model for the woodcut of the palace for the *Secondo Libro*. A very similar drawing that in the same way shows both the façade and court on the same folio exists also for Palazzo Thiene and Palazzo Valmarana.[13]

From the manner of drawing and also from the style in which the statues are composed, we see that the folios must be more or less contemporary, that is to say c. 1566, when Palazzo Valmarana was begun and when Palladio was working on the definitive version of the *Quattro Libri*. At that date Palazzo Porto had certainly been finished for a long time in its present form, therefore the sixth drawing cannot be a plan for it. That the drawing had been utilized by the engraver appears confirmed by the fact that the dimensions of the *Secondo Libro* correspond closely to that of the drawing, even though there are small variations, for example, in the attic windows. In the drawing they are perfectly squared; in the reproduction in the *Secondo Libro* they are instead four by three and three-quarters feet. But it is impossible to determine if such variants had been introduced by the engraver or if they were due to a last-minute intervention by Palladio himself.

Moreover, clear differences between the drawing in question (fig. X) and the building strike the eye. In the drawing of the façade Palladio indicates four wedge-shaped stones above the windows. In the *Secondo Libro* they have become three, and in the building as built they have been increased to five. The fact that in the drawing only one window in the *piano nobile* was adorned with figures and garlands shows only that Palladio left to the engraver the task of completing the design. The statues on the attic present us with a complex problem. One wonders whether in fact the corner figures had been forgotten in the drawing and the engraver added them at the request of Palladio, or if at that point no figures were required there. And what is the significance of the single figure in the drawing that is in front of the small central pilaster of the attic, exactly where we find the statues today? Perhaps it is a question of an error that the engraver corrected. Insofar as the court area is concerned, the engraver in the *Secondo Libro* has not only changed the figures and the balustrade in front of the attic but has taken the liberty of repeating in the ground floor the projecting stone surfaces of the façade instead of the windows with moldings according to Palladio's drawing. Since the ground floor as it was realized corresponds in general outline to the drawing, its reproduction in the *Secondo Libro* must be imputed to the imagination of the en-

graver, unless Palladio himself made the change for some reason unknown to us.

Thus the evidence provided by the incongruences between the sixth drawing, the woodcut in the *Secondo Libro*, and the actual building is not very significant. The number and the placement of the statues in front and above the attic cannot be related with any assurance to the true intentions of Palladio, the more so if they were not drawn by him. What the architect wished and what he added must be deduced principally from the building itself.

NOTES TO CHAPTER II

[1] This collection will be cited as R.I.B.A. The drawings of Palazzo Porto are found in volumes XVI and XVII. ZORZI, 1965, pp. 187 ff., at times went back to other drawings. The plans, plates 159 and 163 in Zorzi, do not refer, in my opinion, to Palazzo Porto, nor do the sketches of various façades, plate 164.

[2] See ZORZI, 1965, pls. 17 and 18.

[3] For the early villas see ZORZI, 1968, pp. 39 ff., and BARBIERI, 1970.

[4] The well-known drawing of the Casa di Raffaello in the R.I.B.A. collection is not actually by Palladio, but was in his possession (see ZORZI, 1959, pl. 304).

[5] The right side of the drawing has been related to Palazzo Pojana al Corso in Vicenza, certainly without plausible justification, since the drawing is a youthful work while the palace of Vincenzo Pojana was begun only around 1560. The similarities

derive from the type and not from the Palladian design. See ZORZI, 1965, p. 297.

[6] ALBERTI, 1565, bk. I, chapter 13, p. 34.

[7] PALLADIO, 1570, *Primo Libro*, chapter XXVIII: "Delle Scale, e varie maniere di quelle, e del numero, e grandezza de' gradi." Palladio certainly knew *L'Architettura di Pietro Cataneo*, Venice, 1554, in which the stairway is already defined as "more difficult and important than anything" (in the *Quattro Libri*, p. 96).

[8] "Dell'Atrio testugginato, e della Casa privata degli Antichi Romani," bk. II, chapter VII.

[9] Cited by ZORZI, 1959, pp. 183 ff.

[10] [MUTTONI], 1740, vol. I, p. 8.

[11] "Delle case private de' Greci," bk. II, chapter XI.

[12] ZORZI, 1965, p. 192.

[13] ZORZI, 1965, pls. 213 and 300.

III

THE EXTERIOR AND INTERIOR
OF THE PALACE

The present façade of the palace (figs. 4 and *a*), is the result of repeated renovations. The two-headed eagle which can be seen in eighteenth century engravings and also in an 1842 lithograph by Marco Moro (fig. XXIII) has disappeared from the portal. Before we can grasp the grandiose conception of the façade, we must overcome a moment of perplexity and a first impression almost of disappointment; the palace is located in a narrow street and can be examined at a distance only with difficulty (fig. 3). When standing directly in front of it, the high ground floor with its long flat base and its flattened rustication gives the impression of repulsing the visitor more than any other Palladian palace (fig. 5). The effect is intentional; this façade was a screen the owner used to separate himself from the vulgar world. The great dimensions reduce the passerby to a modest size. The rusticated stone gives the building a heroic character suitable to public buildings or habitations of the nobility, not to a middle-class dwelling.[1] The masks (figs. 8 and 9) in the keystones of the arches above the windows also contribute to this effect. Some have a tragic aspect and some are crowned with exotic headdresses. They are inspired by the "Persians," the prisoners of the Spartans of whom Vitruvius speaks in the first chapter of the *Primo Libro*. They are thus warlike symbols and appear often in the architecture of the cinquecento, either in full figure, that is, as herms, or as masks alone. The heads of Palazzo Porto have unquestionable similarities with those of Palazzo Cordellina in Contra' Riale or with Palazzo Loschi Zileri Dal Verme, both works in Vicenza by Calderari. Although the masks appear in the illustration of the palace in the *Secondo Libro*, it is also possible that they were remade during Calderari's time. In any case these faces (figs. 20-25), which are almost portraits, are clearly different from cinquecentesque masks like those on the Basilica Palladiana.[2]

The ground floor provides a contrast with the *piano nobile*, which is more splendid and less severe. The latter (fig. 7) is articulated by the Ionic order, an order that lies between Doric simplicity and Corinthian pomp and one that Palladio especially loved.[3] The half-columns rest on the upper edge of the ground floor so that the wall of the *piano nobile* seems to be set back a little (scale drawing IX). The columns, including the base and the capital, should have a height measuring their diameter times nine, in conformity with chapter XVI of the *Primo Libro*. In fact, they are a little shorter, as the plans show. The seven windows (figs. 12-16) are crowned by pediments that are alternately triangular and segmental and that rest on volutes. The decoration of the windows conforms to the rules that Palladio himself gave in chapter XXVI of the *Primo Libro*: "Concerning the ornaments of doors and windows." A tripartite architrave runs around the opening and above it is a frieze or a cornice. In this, Palladio is inspired by the precepts of Vitruvius.

The contrast between the powerful ground floor and the lighter *piano nobile* is also underlined by the window balusters, which allow light to penetrate the solid wall. For these balusters Palladio adopted a Bramantesque form that also appears in other palaces of the cinquecento. They mark "a bilateral symmetry of the two column shafts." They are slender and stand out from one another so decisively that they form a distinct screen in front of the windows.[4] In contrast with Casa Civena where the window frontals are made up of an ornamental fretwork, the balustrades of Palazzo Porto represent a step toward maturity. They enter into the play of the plastic forms of the façade, combining to create the chiaroscuro of the general conception.

The reclining figures above the windows (figs. 12-14) can be attributed to an artist in the circle of Alessandro Vittoria, but certainly not to Vittoria himself, since they do not approach the quality of similar figures of the Sala degli Dei in Palazzo Thiene, which are actually by Vittoria.[5] Their author might very well be Vittoria's brother-in-law, Lorenzo Rubini, who in 1553 worked with him in Venice and in 1556 took up permanent residence in Vicenza.[6] Until his death in 1574, Rubini executed stuccoes and sculptures for Palladio's buildings. The slender and elongated figures with their uncertain anatomy, with their small heads and rather sleepy eyes, are characteristic of the style of Rubini, as is the heavy drapery with few folds. Similar figures appear in Palazzo

Porto Barbaran and in the Loggia del Capitanio. The attic with its pilasters and squared windows is very simple.[7] In Palladio's preparatory drawings it did not appear to be decorated with figures. Only in the drawing R.I.B.A. XVII, 3, and in the *Secondo Libro*, as we have seen, do allegorical figures appear. As in all the Palladian palaces they were statues in the round, and were set above the pilasters. Moreover, only four of the eight figures were put in place, so that the whole arrangement appears temporary.

Probably all four figures represent famous individuals of the Porto family. Two are identifiable, thanks to the inscription on the pedestal: IOSEPH PORTIUS, the patron, and LEONIDA PORTIUS, the heir to the palace (figs. 26 and 27). They wear the classic military cloak. Iseppo appears as an old man, Leonida as a beardless youth. Although the figures are idealized and cannot be understood as portraits, the sculptor nevertheless showed that in the figure of Iseppo he had tried for a clear likeness to the subject. The physical structure and the broad face with the high forehead bring to mind the portrait by Veronese. The two anonymous figures (figs. 29 and 30) are more slender, but are undoubtedly by the same studio.

As I have already said, the four sculptures must have been executed and placed *in situ* after the version of the palace that we see in the *Secondo Libro*, about or a little after 1570, but when Iseppo was still alive, since Leonida would not have had himself represented as a youth, given the fact that at the time of the death of his father in 1580 he had already been married for a decade and was over thirty years old. These four statues also reveal a clear tie with the style of Vittoria, especially the old bearded man on the left (fig. 29), but they are crude in execution. If we consider the sculpture of Vicenza of this period, we

XII - Andrea Palladio, *Front elevation of Palazzo da Porto Festa*. From *I Quattro Libri dell'Architettura*, Venice, 1570, II, chapter III, p. 9

can cite in comparison the allegorical figures in the pronaos of the Rotonda. They have in fact the same slightly articulated anatomy, the same wan faces with sleepy eyes, the same hard and compact drapery. The sculptures of the Rotonda are, according to the testimony of Palladio himself, "by Messer Lorenzo of Vicenza, a most excellent sculptor,"[8] and for that reason also the statues of Palazzo Porto could be attributed to Lorenzo Rubini. Since he died in 1574, the statues of Palazzo Porto could be among his last works, executed perhaps in collaboration with his two sons, Virgilio and Agostino.

Entering the palace, we find ourselves in a tetrastyle atrium (figs. 31-36) that Palladio described in chapter V of the *Secondo Libro*. Palladio had repeatedly used atria or similar rooms in his palaces and villas,[9] for example, in Palazzo Thiene in which a pictoral element in the rustic columns predominates. In Palazzo Porto, on the other hand, the atrium is severely Doric and decisively monumental. An atrium of this type has also a precise structural function, since with its columns it supports the upper-floor rooms. In part it is a characteristic element of the ancient house and thus symbolically also upholds the dignity of the patron. It was built in accordance with the original plan and the bases, capitals, cornices, moldings, niches, and pilasters form a complex whole, that is balanced by the Doric simplicity of the details (figs. 37 and 38) and by the largeness of scale. Since the façade of the ground floor was of an almost Doric simplicity, the atrium is in perfect relationship with the external façade. The four freestanding columns with their plain shafts allowed Palladio to create a grandiose space that serves to reecho and almost to intensify the prevalent chiaroscuro of the façade. In the *Secondo Libro* the tetrastyle atrium of the ancient Romans has a coffered ceiling and an impluvium. In Palazzo Porto, on the other hand, the ceiling is covered by a groin vault that is supported by the four columns. There are four recessed panels or coffers at the corners while at the sides the vault's curve is uninterrupted. Since each roundheaded arch is flanked by two trabeations we have the effect of the Serlian motif with the acquisition of spatial value (figs. 33 and 34). A section of the atrium makes the genesis of this space evident (scale drawing VII). Palladio has here created a completely new spatial form that in type is derived from the Vitruvian tetrastyle atrium, but which, through fusion with the modern device, the Serlian motif, is radically transformed. It is introduced not as an easy expedient but as the fruit of a new sense of spatial values. No architect before Palladio created an entrance so harmonic and at the same time so monumental. Interesting in this context is the correspondence with the entrance of Michelangelo's Laurentian Library.

Michelangelo, almost by necessity, inserted architectonic elements in the walls, while Palladio liberated them from the walls by accentuating their autonomy and conferring upon them structural and formal dignity.

The short gallery that follows the atrium was changed from the original design by opening up doorways leading to the small rooms at the corners of the gallery. On entering the court, it is immediately apparent that nothing of the great peristyle was built. The wooden model of the palace, made with extreme accuracy for the Palladian Exhibition of 1973, helps to give us the impression of how the space of the great peristyle, as it was developed between the two blocks of the palace, would have looked (figs. 40-42). Passing through the loggia and looking toward the court we observe the double value that it would have assumed: as a passage between the two houses and at the same time as the center of the whole organism (fig. 43).

Unfortunately, in its present state the wall facing the court (fig. 39) is regrettably, incomplete. The disposition of the windows and their width correspond to what we see in the drawing R.I.B.A. XVII, 3. The rustication in the ground floor that we see in the engraving of the *Secondo Libro* is missing. The balustrade in front of the central window is the only decorative element and is identical to the balustrades of the façade in front. If one wanted to build the peristyle in accordance with the design of the *Secondo Libro*, it could be done with little change in the present façade of the court (scale drawing VI).

On the ground floor the spaces to the left of the atrium and the gallery in the complex correspond to the plan. The rooms in the right section, as well as the whole *piano nobile*, were changed in the nineteenth century so that they are no longer in accord with Palladio's concept.

In 1845 Magrini wrote that the *piano nobile* "recently has been ruined in the internal distribution of its parts."[10] We therefore may date the transformation of Palladio's space in the present rotunda (fig. 85) to shortly before 1845, when the proprietor of the palace was Orazio Guardino Colleoni-Porto, who was married to Caterina Roncalli.[11] Since, as we know from Palladio's description in the Correr manuscript, the depth and length of the room were calculated on the basis of a relationship to the diagonal, if one assumes that the rotunda and the small rooms toward Contra' Porti had been enclosed within the walls of the original room, then in accordance with the new elevations a more or less precise proportion of 2:3 would have resulted. But since

we do not have any original drawings of the *piano nobile* it is impossible to determine the actual state of the original room.

This loss is certainly to be deplored, but it cannot be denied that the new rotunda offers, in the taste of late Neoclassicism, an impression of remarkable grandiosity. Its diameter measures ten meters. The cupola is a hemisphere five meters in height including the cornice. Since the total height from the floor to the top of the cupola is not ten but thirteen meters, the lofty space corresponds more to the salon in Palladio's Villa Rotonda than to the internal space of the Pantheon (scale drawing VII). In its position in the center of the house and in its dimensions it also corresponds to the salon in Villa Rotonda. Perhaps it is not an accident that in the frieze between the wall and the cupola (figs. 87-90), where the four Arts are represented, we see a drawing of that famous villa. The new room would therefore be a Neoclassical interpretation of that illustrious model.

In the frieze of the rotunda, the putti that represent sculpture are busy making a double relief portrait that probably portrays Orazio Colleoni-Porto and Caterina Roncalli (fig. 89). All of the representations of the Arts are in white stucco on a clear blue ground that brings to mind Wedgwood porcelain. The quality of the details is mediocre, but the general appearance has a remarkable decorative effect. The unadorned walls stand out from the frieze. The cupola is coffered and decorated with reliefs in stucco that represent musical instruments (fig. 86). The entire room is thus a homage to the Arts and to the Venetian tradition. The names of the architect and the maker of the stuccoes are not known, but stylistically the room recalls the manner of G. A. Selva and A. Diedo, who constructed the temple of Canova at Possagno, which was finished in 1830, the interior of which also contains a coffered cupola illuminated from above.[12]

The round room does not give the impression of a room to be lived in. Rather it seems to be representative of public architecture, and indeed it was used as such. In 1871 Rumor wrote in his guide: "They are working on the new tribunal, which will occupy the whole *piano nobile* [of Palazzo Porto]. Magnificent halls and rooms with paintings, stuccoes, damasks, and really good substantial objects.... The proprietors, heirs, the counts Giuseppe Porto will turn over all the said floor and the top story." And on 30 November of the same year: "Solemn opening of the Criminal Court of Vicenza with the participation of the National Guard. The site for this Tribunal is in Contra' Porti in the palace of the Countess Irene Porto."

At that time there were still numerous paintings on the *piano nobile* that had been gathered together in the palace for more than three centuries, but certainly the frescoes by Veronese, of which Muttoni spoke, were no longer in place: "In the two lateral rooms of the Ceremonial Hall the frieze paintings and the overmantel paintings are by the hand of the ever-famous Paolo Caliari, called Veronese. And because of the passage of time and other calamities they have lost some of their original beauty and are now being restored by the noblewoman Countess Maddalena Angarana Porto."[13] The works by Veronese, which around 1740, when Muttoni wrote his description, must already have been restored, fell into such neglect in the hundred years that followed that the meager vestiges remaining were eliminated during the restoration of 1845. Since Palladio did not mention Veronese in the Correr manuscript, but spoke of

him in the printed text, the friezes and the overmantel paintings by Veronese must have been executed between 1565 and 1570. In the salon, moreover, according to a description by Arnaldi, there once were works by P. Liberi, Balante da Thiene, and Piazzetta, which now are lost.[14] The small circular room, three meters in diameter, in the southeast corner of the palazzo on the *piano nobile*, which has a cupola decorated with nineteenth-century Pompeian motifs (the work of an unknown artist of the same period) belongs to the restoration of 1845 (fig. 84). Whoever passes through the *piano nobile* of Palazzo Porto today finds himself immersed in the characteristic atmosphere of the late Neoclassicism of the past century, as does the visitor entering the many smaller rooms that were adapted to offices during the twentieth-century remodernization (scale drawing IV).

In 1954 the rooms of the ground floor were restored. In 1959 the atrium was replastered. In 1968 the *piano nobile* was restored again, while minor repairs were carried out on the stuccoes and the cupola. In 1971 the façade was recovered with new plaster, the tonality of which adhered as closely as possible to the original color of the cinquecento. At the same time, the damaged parts of the figures and the garlands of the *piano nobile* were restored and completed by Giuseppe Giacometti. The restoration was made very obvious so that in examining the decoration close up it is easily recognized. This work was executed under the Sovrintendenza ai Monumenti of Venice and directed by the architect Luigi Pavan.[15] Aside from the modifications carried out in the eighteenth and nineteenth centuries, Porto Festa is today Palladio's best preserved palace.

NOTES TO CHAPTER III

[1] In the circle of sixteenth-century Venetian architects it was principally Sanmicheli who gave this allegorical significance to rustication, for example, in the gates of Verona. In Udine, Palladio utilized this type of strongly rusticated surface for Palazzo Antonini, while the rustication of Palazzo Porto appears more drawn than modeled. However, the nineteenth-century restoration may have changed the early conception.

[2] Compare figs. 51-62 in BARBIERI, 1968, with the masks of Palazzo Porto. The masks of the Basilica to some extent resemble lions' heads and are at the same time stylized as ornaments. For the dating of the masks of Palazzo Porto, whether they are sixteenth or eighteenth century, we have as yet no documents. ZORZI, 1965, p. 194, would be inclined to ascribe the masks to Alessandro Vittoria. He defined them as "caricature-like," which in the language of the cinquecento corresponds to grotesques. But this interpretation also is incorrect; the masks of Palazzo Porto represent individualized faces and are not grotesque ornaments.

[3] In the years around 1550 Palladio used the Ionic order in the *piano nobile* of Palazzo Chiericati and, as the only order, in the villas Foscari at Malcontenta, Badoer at Fratta Polesine, and Barbaro at Maser.

[4] WITTKOWER, 1968, pp. 332 ff.

[5] MAGAGNATO, 1966, figs. 93 ff.

[6] ZORZI, 1951, V, pp. 141 ff. On the stucco workers and sculptors who worked on the Palladian buildings, especially Bartolomeo Ridolfi and Lorenzo and Agostino Rubini, we still do not have monographs. Consequently, at the present time we are restricted to working on attributions that are more or less secure. The best documented study of the various workshops of Vicenza is found in BARBIERI, 1968, in the chapter "La decorazione scultorea," pp. 101 ff. Lorenzo Rubini worked on the Basilica in the years 1550-52, but we do not know whether the decorations of the windows in Palazzo Porto were already in place in those years or only after 1556.

[7] As the new drawings demonstrate, the windows of the attic are actually square, as in Palladio's drawing R.I.B.A. XVII, 3, and not rectangular as in the *Secondo Libro*.

[8] *Secondo Libro*, p. 18. Cf. SEMENZATO, 1968, p. 34, on the decorative function of the figures of Lorenzo Rubini and of their ideal relation with the architecture of Palladio. See also SEMENZATO, 1968, pls. 12-16. Since the statues of the Rotonda, which must have been put in place a little before 1570, reveal great stylistic similarities with those of Palazzo Porto, my thesis that the "portraits" of the da Portos must be late works by Lorenzo Rubini would seem to be acceptable.

[9] PRINZ, 1969, XI, pp. 370 ff., and FORSSMAN, 1965, pp. 64 ff. The ancient house had an open atrium, something that for practical and traditional reasons could not be introduced into a modern palace. In his *Commento a Vitruvio*, BARBARO, 1556, bk. VI, chapter IV, p. 172, said: "The Atrium is that part one first enters on coming into the house; it is a covered place, and in the middle is the principal door, and on the opposite side are the doors that lead to the Peristyles." This identification of the atrium with the entrance hall of the modern house is exactly what we find in Palladio. In regard to the vault, see WILINSKI, 1969, XI, pp. 415 ff.

[10] MAGRINI, 1845, p. 26.

[11] Orazio Colleoni-Porto died 7 December 1848. For information about him I wish to thank dott. Antonio Cian of the Vicenza State Archives.

[12] In this connection Franco Barbieri kindly suggested to me that for the stuccoes in the rotunda of the palace the name of Antonio Bagutti of Lugano might be proposed. A contemporary source stated that he was "very deeply versed in the art of making stuccoes, having from 1802 a fixed residence in our city; he surpassed all others in the many contracts for work he made with the richest families of Vicenza." (TRISSINO, 1856, p. 21.)

[13] [MUTTONI], 1740, vol. I. There does not seem to be any information in the Palladian literature about the decoration of the large room toward Contra' Porti.

[14] ARNALDI ET AL., 1779, pp. 82 ff. In Palazzo Porto stood out "five paintings with figures of the goddess Venus, all in different poses, singular works by Cavalier Liberi. The two small paintings over the two doors are by Piazzetta." And further on: "In a lower mezzanine there are four large paintings by Balante da Thiene, a pupil of Cavalier Liberi, representing riding horses and other things for the hunt and equitation." We note that the hunt is also the theme of the panels painted by Tiepolo in the small room near the corridor; in that regard see below.

[15] I am indebted to dott. Manlio Sanmartin for the dates. The plaster, which was not suitable to the spirit of the building, covered the façade of the palace until 1971 and must have been applied around 1820, since in BERTI, 1822, it is noted that the façade was finished and restored a few years earlier.

a) - Palazzo da Porto Festa: façade seen from the left

b) - DOMENICO BRUSASORZI: *The Fall of the Giants*, detail (fresco on the vault of the square room on the ground floor)

c) - Domenico Brusasorzi: *The Fall of the Giants*, detail (fresco on the vault of the square room on the ground floor)

IV

THE SIGNIFICANCE OF PALAZZO PORTO IN THE WORK OF PALLADIO AND IN THE HISTORY OF ARCHITECTURE

Before his voyage to Rome in 1541 Palladio planned Casa Civena, still influenced by Falconetto and Sanmicheli, that is, by Venetian Bramantism, which at that time was no longer completely modern. We do not know what particularly interested Palladio during his first Roman journey, which was very brief.[1] It is likely that above all he studied the most recent architecture. Bramante and Raphael were long dead and their most famous works were by then "classic" in the sense of a prototype that is beyond question. But their taste had been developed and modified by Antonio da Sangallo, Peruzzi, and others. Palladio understood at that time that Venetian and Roman Bramantism were completely different manifestations of the same thing. The dimensions that Roman architecture achieved were much greater, beyond any human scale. It was clear that the columns were not just a decorative element but also structural entities with which spaces could be created, as in the atrium of Palazzo Farnese. The intercolumniations not only articulate variable intervals but also emphasize well-defined tensions, as we can see in Palazzo Massimo. Moreover, the wall in Rome took on different characteristics than it did in the Veneto. It was not a smooth background on which decorations and ornaments could be applied, but, like the walls of the Palazzo Farnese courtyard, it resembled the skin of a body through which muscles stand out. Every detail, as in Bramante's Belvedere Court, was in a reciprocal and indissoluble relationship with the whole. A building was not limited, as in the Veneto, to a façade with spaces behind, but took shape in the form of a very solid rectangular block that a person could walk around, the center of which became the court enclosed by arcades, as was the case in the Cancelleria.

When Palladio returned to the Veneto he thought of putting in practice something of his Roman experiences. His first great undertaking was the plan for Palazzo Thiene, which I believe may be dated 1542, even though the construction must have been started a little later. It reveals the attempt to introduce the Roman-Florentine type of palace into the Veneto. It had to encompass an entire block and introduce a great square arcaded court. Like Palazzo Farnese, it was to have two counterposed colonnaded atria that led directly into the court without a tablinum or gallery. On the outside there are features reminiscent of the Cancelleria. In fact, local influences, derived from Giulio Romano and Sanmicheli, are seen in the details. If the palace had been finished it would be the only manifestation of a truly Roman architecture outside of Rome. At the same time it is understandable that it remained unfinished, since the Roman palace did not correspond in any way to the concept that the Venetian nobles had of a residence. It was simply too big, it extended over too much space, and it had a too-diffuse system of communications. The people of Venice and Vicenza lived in houses in which the rooms were arranged in long rows and in direct contact with the *portego* that served as the axis and means of communication between all the areas. Sanmicheli had already accepted that type of habitation, but now, with Palazzo Thiene, Palladio wished to make a break with tradition and impose on the people of Vicenza a Roman model, to build spaces for them that they did not accept and to lay out internal arrangements that they did not want.

Perhaps soon after the beginning of the work, it became clear that Palazzo Thiene would be a mistake. For that reason when he drafted the first plan for Palazzo Porto, Palladio returned to the Venetian tradition. Such a choice cannot have been made just because of the particular shape of the land available, since Palazzo Massimo, for example, is also on a relatively narrow plot facing the street, and is nevertheless a palace in the Roman style. Palladio instead oriented the palace toward a *portego* that imposed an arrangement of the rooms on the two sides of a central axis on both of the two floors. He did not want, however, to give up his Roman experiments altogether. In the introduction to the "Disegni delle case della città" (Designs for City Houses) in the *Secondo Libro* he stated in this regard "how difficult it is to introduce a new style, especially in building, a profession in which everyone is convinced that he has knowledge."[2] What was the "new style" that he introduced into Venetian architecture with Palazzo Porto? It consists of a synthesis of the modern Roman style, the

ancient classical tradition, and Venetian custom.

Let us consider once again the façade of the palace (fig. 5). The artist wished to define it vertically throughout the three stories: the ground floor with shallow rustication, the *piano nobile* articulated by the engaged columns of the Ionic order, and the concluding attic story. Such a sequence derives from Roman architecture. It represents that brief state of Roman Bramantism that Palladio was evidently still following, but that Roman architecture itself was about to discard. Certainly Venetian architecture had for some time known of façades adorned with columns. Palazzo Vendramin by Mauro Coducci on the Grand Canal had columns on the façade even before they appeared on Roman façades, and Palazzo Corner and Palazzo Dolfin by Sansovino already showed the motif in a manner more in conformity with the Vitruvian rules. Sanmicheli used it more rigorously in Palazzo Pompei. But, analogous to the Roman model, it appears for the first time in Palladio's work in Palazzo Porto. A single order truly dominates the façade, and the unadorned shafts of the columns dispel the impression that they are purely decorative, as they seem in all the preceding examples in the Veneto. Since a façade of a Venetian palace could not appear to be "ascetic," Palladio also turned toward Sansovino when he wished to decorate the windows with reclining figures and garlands and, in sum, to give the façade a more lively play of light and shade, as Venetian taste now demanded.

In the development of the plan he introduced the new style still more decisively. Changing the *portego* into a Vitruvian atrium and the court into a peristyle, he made the Venetian house correspond to ancient Roman houses. What Palladio would say later of the Convento della Carità is valid also for

XIII - ANDREA PALLADIO, *Elevation on the courtyard of Palazzo da Porto Festa.* From *I Quattro Libri dell'Architettura*, Venice, 1570, II, chapter III, p. 10

Palazzo Porto: "I tried to make this house like those of the Ancients."[3] But Palladio knew the mansions of the ancient Romans only from Vitruvius's description (fig. XVIII) and from Alberti. Palazzo Porto therefore is not an imitation of the Roman house, but an original reinterpretation made on the basis of the ancient sources. It reveals an early phase of research done by Palladio in order to give to the Venetian nobles a residence that was classic and modern, grandiose and livable.

For the first time in the history of architecture he used the giant order in a court. Since Vitruvius's house was on one floor, Palladio could not find anything in Vitruvius on which to base the concept of a court rising up two or three stories.

Where then did he get the stupendous idea for his colossal peristyle? Bertotti Scamozzi has correctly pointed out the source for this court. It is to be found in the reconstruction made by Barbaro and Palladio himself of the Vitruvian basilica at Fano,[4] the central nave of which had great Corinthian columns, while the loggias were supported by pilasters placed behind the columns. Here the balusters also are joined directly to the shafts of the columns. Assuming that the peristyle had been introduced in the course of the planning, since the drawings in London show a court without colonnades, then the peristyle of the palace and the reconstruction of the Vitruvian basilica might have been invented at the same time, at the beginning of the 1550s, that is, after Palladio had begun his collaboration with Daniele Barbaro in the translation of Vitruvius. In the meantime the artist had visited Rome repeatedly, something that could not help but have consequences for the planning of Palazzo Porto.

The interior decorations (discussed below) also correspond to antique conceptions. From this time Palladio always

spoke of the "very beautiful stuccoes" and the "most excellent paintings" in the descriptions of his houses. Moreover, there was the testimony of Vitruvius and of the Domus Aurea to demonstrate that the rooms of the ancient Romans were adorned with sculpture, stuccoes, and frescoes. The Renaissance did not want to do anything different. The function of such decoration can be defined as "manneristic" insofar as the style is concerned. It achieved, according to Vasari, "more completely elegant elegance" producing "that third style that we like to call modern."[5] The exterior of Palazzo Porto therefore still takes its point of departure from concepts of the Renaissance, whereas the contrast between the imposing façade and the richly adorned interior is to be understood as the modern manner or, as we now say, Mannerism.[6]

The first citation of Palazzo Porto is found in the 1568 Vasari, in which the author said that he did not think there could be a building "either more magnificent, or more beautiful, or more worthy of any great prince than it is."[7] Scamozzi, on the other hand, naturally omitted any discussion of it. An extensive comment on the palace is found in manuscript in the copy of the *Quattro Libri* owned by the great English architect Inigo Jones. It reveals that Jones studied the palace with special care. He noted the date of his visit (18 January 1614) and also the fact that the palace was built entirely of brick. He made further annotations on 2 June 1632, thus demonstrating how long he remained interested in this subject.[8] Moreover, he probably possessed the drawings for Palazzo Porto that are now in London.[9] A consequence of Jones's interest can be seen in his Queen's House in Greenwich, a work of 1616-35, in which he introduced rustication on the ground floor and an Ionic order *piano nobile*, although

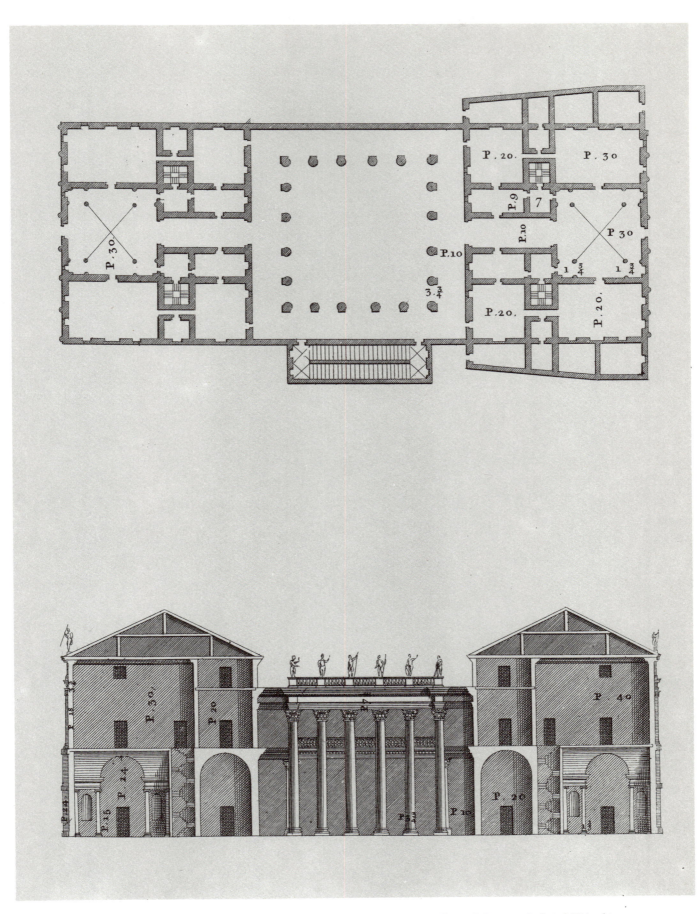

XIV - Isaac Ware, *Ground plan and section of Palazzo da Porto Festa*. From *I Quattro Libri dell'Architettura*, London, 1738, I, pl. IV

with a completely original interpretation.

In France we note a remarkable interest in Palladio in the middle of the seicento. In 1650 there appears the translation of the *Quattro Libri* by Fréart de Chambray.[10] As for Louis Levau, we do not know whether he visited the Veneto, but in 1667 he adopted an arrangement for the garden façade of the Palace of Versailles that cannot derive from any source other than the illustration of Palazzo Porto in the *Secondo Libro*. A rusticated ground floor with masks on the projections supports an Ionic order *piano nobile* with balusters on the windows and, above, an attic with pilasters, in front of which are statues. Although characteristic elements of the French Baroque appear — windows with roundheaded arches in the *piano nobile*, and the alternation of pilasters and columns instead of engaged columns — the source is indisputable.

In the eighteenth century English Palladianism derives many of its elements from Palazzo Porto. In his *Vitruvius Britannicus* of 1715 Colin Campbell designed for English noblemen two palaces that, with their rusticated ashlar ground floors and their Ionic *piano nobiles*, have clear similarities with Palazzo Porto.[11] The façade of Burlington House in London, rebuilt in 1719 by the famous Palladianist Lord Burlington, was also modeled after Palazzo Porto. The building was appreciably altered in the nineteenth century when it became the seat of the Royal Academy, but it still recalls its Vicentine origin. In England, as in France, there were free variations of the Vicentine palace. For these, if it is improper to speak of imitations, it is correct to say that Palazzo Porto was the model for many free derivations.

The first complete edition of the *Quattro Libri*, which the Venetian Giacomo Leoni published in London in 1716-20 with English, French, and Italian texts, was of great importance for English Palladianism.[12] As early as 1721 an English edition was brought out. In Leoni's work we find copper engravings of Palazzo Porto made in Holland by Picart. They are copies derived from the *Secondo Libro* with some changes. Thus Leoni, misunderstanding the artist's thought, introduced a correction. Although in the drawing of the court Palladio had interrupted the Corinthian trabeation with small arches over each intercolumniation in order to give more light to the upper floor (fig. XIII), Leoni, not having fully comprehended the author's idea, drew an uninterrupted trabeation (fig. XX). The most beautiful and most exact English edition is that of 1738 by Isaac Ware. And Ware reproduced the court correctly, with the trabeation interrupted by small arches, in correspondence with the two sections of the palace (figs. XIV and XV).

The most important of the great eighteenth century editions of Palladio for us is Muttoni's *Architettura* in which Palazzo Porto appears in the fifth volume, which was published in 1744.[13] It is disappointing, however, to see that the plates by Muttoni (fig. XVI) are only copies derived from Leoni's edition of Palladio. Even the statues of the attic and of the court are copied. Muttoni's engraver, Giorgio Fossati, however, restored the trabeation of the court to the form indicated by Palladio in the *Secondo Libro* and corrected its measurements (fig. XIX). Muttoni's text provides, as we have seen, some important information on Palazzo Porto.

Subsequently, in 1762, the palace was mentioned by Temanza, to whom we are also indebted for the date of construction of 1552. "Count Giuseppe Porto was perhaps among the first of the citizens of Vicenza who availed themselves of the work of our Architect" and the result was

XV - Isaac Ware, *Front elevation of Palazzo da Porto Festa*. From *The Four Books of Andrea Palladio's Architecture*, London, 1738, I, pl. V

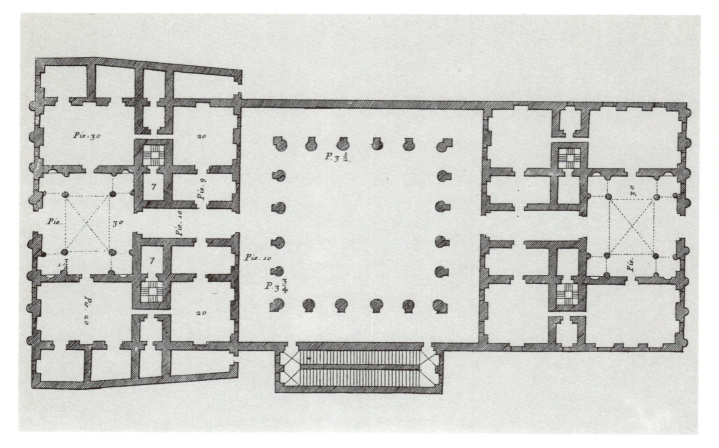

XVI - FRANCESCO MUTTONI, *Plan of Palazzo da Porto Festa.* From *Architettura di Andrea Palladio Vicentino.*
Venice, 1744, V, pl. V

a "fine indication of his good taste."[14] That was all that he had to say about the palace. A very precise judgment on Palazzo Porto is found in *Forestiere Istruito* of 1761 by Bertotti Scamozzi. "There is no superfluity in it, nor have I seen in the works of Palladio more simplicity than this, blended however with that inseparable grandiosity, which he emphasized in all his works."[15] In the single illustration that shows the whole of the façade, and which for that reason is a novelty with respect to the *Secondo Libro*, the statues are for the first time correctly arranged, although they are incorrectly interpreted as ideal figures rather than personages of the Porto family. In his great work of 1776 Bertotti Scamozzi took up Palazzo Porto more carefully, with the entire façade and the court in sectional drawings (figs. XXI and XXII) and the plans, all of which

is taken from the *Secondo Libro* and not directly from the building, but with measurements that he had personally checked.[16] Perhaps one should not overlook the last eighteenth-century edition of the *Quattro Libri*, that by Mucci (Siena, 1791). The engraving of the palace has a certain dryness that is typical of Neoclassical academicism, but it is executed very exactly (fig. XVII).

In actuality the copper engravings of the eighteenth century, however beautiful they are from the point of view of graphics, are essentially only paraphrases of the woodcuts of 1570 and say little or nothing about Palazzo Porto as it really is. The texts consequently start from the false premise that the illustrations of the *Secondo Libro* with the two equal sections joined reveal the original plan of Palladio. The most important description of the

XVII - ALESSANDRO MUCCI, *Front elevation of Palazzo da Porto Festa.* From *I Quattro Libri dell'Architettura di Andrea Palladio*, Siena, 1791, II, p. 13

palace in the eighteenth century remains that by Arnaldi, which I have already cited. In it he said among other things: "No less elegant than the ground plan is the front elevation, forming a solid and pleasing whole."[17] The sentence well emphasizes the validity of the rustication and the Ionic order. In this we find the explanation for various palaces in Vicenza during the settecento using Palazzo Porto as their model.[18] Palazzo Loschi Zileri on the Corso, the work of Ottone Calderari of 1782, is in fact conceived in its individual formal elements like Palazzo Porto. The central part of the façade is thrown into relief by means of the projection of three intercolumniations, as if the façade of Palazzo Porto had passed through the Baroque and had then been again restored to Neoclassical forms. A combination of motifs from Palazzo Porto and Palazzo Porto Barbaran is found in Palazzo Cordellina in Contra' Riale, which was designed in 1774, again by Calderari. Calderari's pupils also studied Palazzo Porto and modified its fundamental elements. Palazzo Fioccardo, now Palazzo de' Troi, by Carlo Barrera has five intercolumniations and a mezzanine on the ground floor, but it is based on Palazzo Porto.

The same arrangement is shown in Palazzo Franco in Corso Padova, a work done in 1830 by Antonio Piovene, which adheres even more to the Palladian model. It must be emphasized that in 1845 Magrini still spoke of "architecture that is modern and Palladian,"[19] and among the oldest examples of it he included Palazzo Porto. Therefore, for the distinguished Vicentine historian, the "modern" architecture initiated by Palladio extends into the middle of the nineteenth century.

What the palace looked like at that time appears clearly in an 1842 lithograph by Marco Moro in which the Contra' Porti is populated by figures in the Austrian Biedermeier manner (fig. XXIII). The reproduction of the façade is more realistic than it is in all the preceding engravings.[20] Moro showed the palace before the restoration of 1845, a result of which was to make the interior of the palace "modern": no longer Palladian, but Neoclassical. In the most recent monographs on Palladio, Palazzo Porto has of course been discussed many times, although none of the authors has attributed a fundamental significance to it.[21] In the critical investigation here, I will try to pinpoint three aspects of the building: the system of the proportions, the problem of the classical vocabulary, and the sociological significance of the palace.

In the drawings in the *Secondo Libro*, Palladio always indicated measurements in Vicentine feet and these measurements must express the proportions of the rooms. For that reason the entire arrangement was related to that "universal harmony" that also played a role in architecture by means of numbers. The proportions of the plan are very simple. The principal rooms are square or have a relationship of 2 : 3 between width and length. Such a relationship corresponds to the fifth interval or diapente in ancient musical theory. It was believed that identical numerical relationships were harmonically valid in music for the ear and in architecture for the eye.[22] The largest room, to the left of the entrance with the vault by Tiepolo, is proportioned in accordance with the diapente, since it measures 6.99 x 10.56 meters. That corresponds closely to the proportion of 20 : 30 Vicentine feet, each of which measures 0.3475 meters. The square room with *The Fall of the Giants* is 20 feet in width, but actually it is not perfectly square, being about 7.00 x 7.30 meters according to the new plans (scale drawing III). The room with the vault with stuccoes does not have any measurement that is comprehensible in terms of whole numbers. It measures 2.69 x 7.10 meters; but was intended to be 10 x 20 feet, or taking account of the thickness of the wall, 9 x 20 feet, measurements that in terms of harmonies correspond more or less to an octave.

Since a room has three dimensions, the harmonic values would have to hold true not only for the floor plan but also for the three-dimensional space. From this it follows that the height would also have to be in harmonic relationship with the length and width. On that subject, in chapter XXIII of the *Primo Libro*, which is devoted to the height of rooms, Palladio formulated three modes or rules. In the text regarding Palazzo Porto he said that the height of the rooms beside the entrance, that is, those discussed above, would have to be "in accordance with the last mode of the height of vaults"; that is, the most complex mode. It means that three measurements (*a*, *b*, *c*) correspond harmonically if the central measurement (*b*) is calculated according to the formula

$$\frac{b-a}{a} = \frac{c-b}{c}$$

In fact, Bertotti Scamozzi correctly calculated the height of the room of 20 x 30 feet to the left of the entrance on the basis of the formula

$$\frac{24-20}{20} = \frac{30-24}{30}$$

The proportional mean is therefore 24, so that the room had to be 24 Vicentine feet high, or 8.33 meters. The height from the floor to the ceiling on the ground floor is actually only about 7 meters (scale drawing VIII), a fact that perplexed Bertotti Scamozzi.[23] On the other hand, Palladio said in the section already cited: "There are also other heights of vaults, which do not fall under the rule: and with these the

Architect must be guided by his own judgment, and by necessity." With that statement all rules become relative and judgment alone remains valid.

As we have seen, the proportions in Palazzo Porto do not correspond fully to the harmonic numbers as they are given in the *Secondo Libro*. Thus the question arises with regard to Palazzo Porto, as well as other Palladian buildings, as to whether the whole building is now disharmonic, that is, if the actual measurements that came about through inaccuracies during construction or through contingent necessity have altered the exact relationships. We know now, thanks to the psychology of perception, that the human eye and brain are not capable of grasping the numerical relationships of space. Whether a space seems harmonic or disharmonic to us does not depend on the fact that the plan is actually proportioned in accordance, for example, with the diapente 2:3. What we grasp immediately is the fundamental form — whether it is round, square, or rectangular — and whether the relationships between length, width, and height are balanced. We grasp very long spaces, for example, not as rooms but as corridors, very deep spaces as wells, without dwelling on the numerical relationships that might be present even in spaces so far removed from the normal. We can observe immediately that the room with *The Fall of the Giants* is square, and we note the more or less "normal" height of the cupola, but we do not take into account that the cupola, according to the rules of proportion, should be higher.

Palladio certainly knew all this, otherwise his buildings as they actually are would have driven him to distraction. Nevertheless, the proportions he established could not have been made up merely of facile formulations that could then be cavalierly tossed aside in the realization of

A, Atrio.
B, Tablino.
C, Periſtilio.
D, Saloti Corinthij.
E, Saloti di quattro colonne.
F, Baſilica.
G, Luoghi per la Eſtate.
H, Stanze.
k, Librarie.

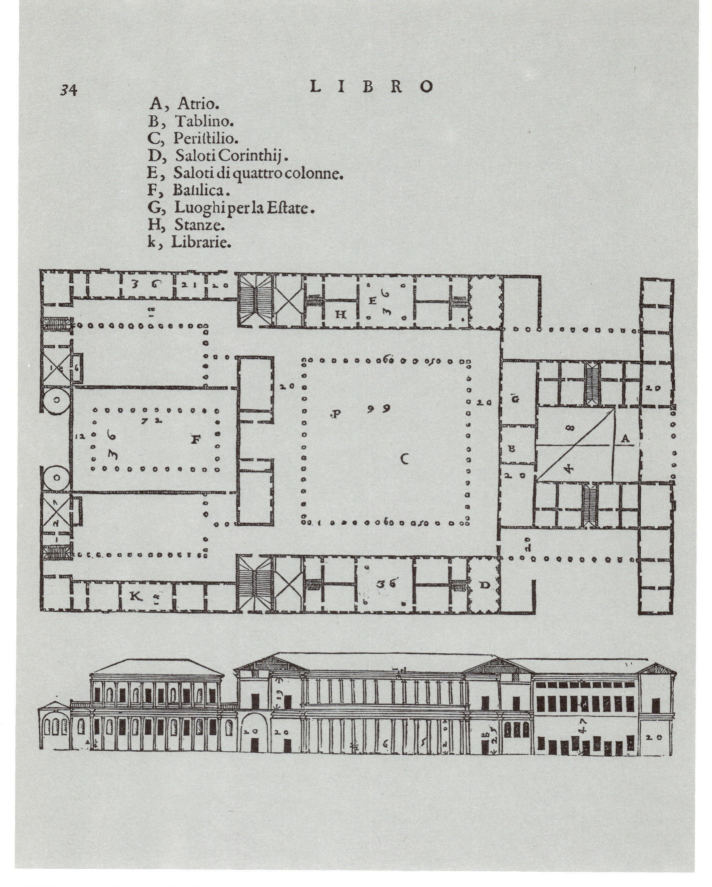

XVIII - ANDREA PALLADIO, *The House of the Ancient Romans.* From *I Quattro Libri dell'Architettura*, II, chapter VII, p. 34

his works. The artist believed in laws that rule the universe and that these laws can be understood by man only through numbers.

Moreover, since God created man in his image and likeness and since every symmetry and proportion, as Vitruvius taught, was derived rationally from man, Palladio could compare a building to "a well-made body." But as one cannot grasp in any given moment in the body of a fine man the aggregate structure, nor note possible small imperfections, so in a building imprecision is not of essential importance for the final result, which can always be modified on the basis of the author's taste or the necessity to which he must at times defer.

The beauty and elegance of Palazzo Porto as it really is — and this Palladio knew as well — consists not in exact measurements, but in something else. Even though we still do not have a precise theory of perception for architecture, we might nevertheless say that our experience, insofar as architecture is concerned, is influenced by significant forms that we consider beautiful and harmonic. This holds true not only for the dimensions and the shapes of the rooms, but also for every detail of the exterior and the interior, for example, for the manner in which the ground floor and the *piano nobile* are differentiated one from the other in the structural context. The windows are actually cutouts in the wall, but optically we grasp them as "shapes" applied to the wall, something that Palladio expressed in his drawings by means of the outlines of the contours. As shapes the windows certainly have significant forms. In Palazzo Porto they are unequivocally vertical rectangles, except for the attic where they are squares and, because of their perfect form, no longer convey an upward tension. The horizontal or vertical sense of forms or parts of a building must be expressed in a clear manner. The ground floor of Palazzo Porto is horizontal, and its horizontal progression is emphasized by the smooth cornices and by the rustication (figs. 8 and 9). The vertical tension of the windows is neutralized by the semicircular arches. The *piano nobile* (fig. 7) has a vertical progression, since here vertical forms predominate. Only the pediments of the windows with the reclining figures, because of their horizontality, prevent the windows from almost breaking against the cornice.

Every form must be either decisively angular or rounded, but it cannot remain indefinite between angular and rounded. That is well demonstrated in the rectangular windows and in the semicircular portal of the ground floor. Here the rhythm is expressed even more simply. A single form, the portal, is accompanied by three forms repeated on the sides: the windows. In other words, each detail of this façade is clear and significant by itself, though at the same time connected to all the other forms in the web of vertical and horizontal elements.

Such beauty can be perceived also in a building of a completely different style, even in a modern building. The beauty of Palazzo Porto does not depend on formulas and classical rules. We can therefore endorse what has been correctly said of Palladio: "His own fidelity to the Vitruvian canons is much more apparent, or, to put it better, more verbal than real."[24] Classicism in Palladio assumes above all the form of the "citation." The Ionic columns, the Corinthian peristyle of Palazzo Porto are citations from ancient architecture, or from Vitruvius, and, independent of the intelligible beauty of the significant form, they create their effect naturally. For that reason these citations have to be very strict, since otherwise they would lose their effectiveness as citations. This ex-

XIX - Francesco Muttoni, *Elevation on the courtyard of Palazzo da Porto Festa*. From *Architettura di Andrea Palladio Vicentino*, Venice, 1744, V, pl. VI

XX - GIACOMO LEONI, *Elevation on the courtyard of Palazzo da Porto Festa*. From *The Architecture of A. Palladio in four books*, London, 1721, II, pl. VII

plains why Palladio changed the classical details so little, and why, compared to Michelangelo, he used so little imagination. The art of citation was cultivated with particular preferences above all by the Mannerists, and for that reason it can be said that the more Palladio repeated in a literal and academic manner the words of Vitruvius so much the greater was his participation in the style of his time, that is to say, in Mannerism. This does not mean that the apparent classicism of Palladio was a form of self-delusion. His admiration for antiquity was genuine, but he was not slavish in his imitation. Thus in some of his villas he could also express himself without reference to antiquity. But when he had to design representative architecture, whether public or private, he could make himself understandable to his contemporaries only in the language of the ancients. His patrons responded solely to such references.

Now we come to Palazzo Porto as a symbol of the social structure of the middle of the cinquecento. What does its classical aspect mean in this context? Recently the classicism of Sansovino was defined as an expression of "state art." When Venice entrusted to him the superintendency of all public buildings, he undertook "to found in Venice a precise vocabulary capable of expressing the universality that the city claims for itself in order to justify its own politics of equilibrium and conservation."[25] This politicization of architecture brought a complete acceptance of classicism in Venice, as is demonstrated by the Library, the Procuratie, and the Loggetta. Such classicism is not a symbol of a style or of an aesthetic evaluation. Rather it is the fruit of an ideological superstructure through which the Republic gave luster to its political reality on the one hand and concealed its true character on the other. Therefore the

language of Sansovino became the official one and, like the political structure in itself, remained bound by strict rules. The dominant aristocratic class made use of this language to identify itself closely with the conservatism of the Republic. From this derived the classicism of the Corner and Dolfin palaces.

Since there are several similarities between these two works by Sansovino and Palazzo Porto, we may ask if even the latter might not be interpreted from the sociopolitical point of view as the symbol of conservatism and — why not? — of the repression exercised by the ruling class in Vicenza. Such an interpretation has been advanced by two young authors who have described Palladio's works as repressive architecture and have judged them to be morally censurable: "On one hand the cultural ideal of the renewal of the antique as the typical phenomenon of the superstructure, on the other hand the complete upheaval of Venetian economics of the cinquecento as the classic phenomenon of the understructure."[26] The new economic structure of Venetian capitalism was the reality of the time, the classicizing style of Palladio the beautiful lie that had to ennoble reality. Therefore Palladio too would have been a reactionary, granted that "his architecture aimed at a perpetuation of the rule of man over man." Consequently, Palladio was inhuman and his villas and palaces a means of repression. Looking at the façade of Palazzo Porto, we might ask ourselves if this recent interpretation could be correct and if we must view the work of Palladio with a sense more of condemnation than of admiration.

It is certainly correct that in Palazzo Porto Palladio wished to make clear the social status of his patron. Indeed the sociologists of today are not the first to understand that forms of architecture are motivated partly by social factors. The *Sesto Libro* of Serlio, for example, discusses "habitations for all classes of men." His drawings begin with simple peasant houses and end with the princely castle. Even the simplest houses are planned with symmetry and thus partake of the idea of beauty. It is important to note, therefore, that symmetry and beauty are not social values, but principles valid for all humanity. The same holds true for spaciousness. In 1548, during the same time in which Palazzo Porto was built, Palladio made drawings for houses in Venice. These plans are for row houses, placed between two small streets,[27] each house made up of an entrance hall and two rooms, one larger than the other, on the ground floor, with a stairway leading to the upper floor where there are two more rooms. Perhaps a modest living room was also contemplated: each set of two houses has a small court with a well in common. The plans of these houses suggest that for the common people Palladio provided very nearly the same conveniences in the disposition of the rooms as he did for the nobles, except that the rooms were smaller in size. Moreover, the arrangement of the various rooms is so modern and practical that the plan could still be followed today for families of modest income. Thus we cannot say that Palladio planned habitations only for aristocrats. However, the Vicentine nobles were his important patrons. Only for them did he build houses with rustication, columns, atrium, and peristyle. Can we then conclude that this was nothing other than an ideological superstructure, revelatory of an inhuman purpose?

Above all I must object to the thesis that Palladio used his architecture to give form to any political ideology. It is a thesis unsupported by proof. On the contrary, his literary works speak against such an interpretation. In the third chapter of the *Secondo Libro* he wrote of how he had been able to convince the patrons of his ideas: "I will be considered most fortunate in having found gentlemen so noble and generous in spirit and so excellent in judgment, who believed in my arguments and abandoned the obsolete practice of building without elegance and without beauty of any sort. And in fact I cannot but greatly thank God (as in all actions we must do), who has helped me so much." We might find a note of irony in these words, as if Palladio wanted to say: "The patrons had the good taste to make my taste their own." Moreover, attention has been drawn to the fact that many of his patrons were attracted to religious heresy and displayed progressive tendencies in the moral and social area,[28] but it is unknown whether Palladio's religious devotion, which appears occasionally in the *Quattro Libri*, was influenced by such tendencies.

The disposition to make himself an instrument of the repressive forces of the society of the time cannot have been present in Palladio, since he could express himself only with the vocabulary of classicism. Should we perhaps turn into an accusation the fact that he built for the Venetian nobles? When Iseppo da Porto turned to him should he have declined the commission or designed a modest house instead of a palace? In reality, ideological criticism does not succeed in providing any clarification of Palladio as a historical phenomenon. History is only that which actually happened and not what might have or could have happened. Important for the history of architecture are the buildings that Palladio actually built, not the decisions he might have taken if he had been a social utopian or one of our contemporaries. In regard to the society of the cinquecento, history long ago expressed its opinions, and it is completely unproductive now to sit in judgment on situations long past. There is, in fact, only one problem and Karl Marx has already formulated it. Why do we experience pleasure from artistic testimonies of social situations that have been transcended? Probably because beauty and dignity are not products of a single social class but concern all humanity.

Palazzo Porto, whose great dignity was obviously originally linked to the social position of the noble Vicentine gentleman, in the course of its many centuries of history has taken on diverse functions and purposes. Today it is judged above all on its aesthetic merits: a wonderful monument made by a unique creative personality.

NOTES TO CHAPTER IV

[1] The chronology of Palladio's voyage to Rome is found in ZORZI, 1959, pp. 15 ff.

[2] PALLADIO, *Secondo Libro*, chapter III, p. 4.

[3] PALLADIO, *Secondo Libro*, chapter VI, p. 29.

[4] The description is found in the first volume of BERTOTTI SCAMOZZI, 1776: "It seems that our architect utilized the weight-bearing pilasters behind the columns after the manner of those of the basilica of Fano, designed by Vitruvius, which held up the framework of the porch of the basilica." Palladio used engaged columns also for the court of Villa Sarego at Santa Sofia, which was designed around 1560.

[5] VASARI, 1568, vol. 3, p. 380 (introduction to the third part).

[6] MAGAGNATO, 1966, p. 16, arrived at the same conclusion in regard to Palazzo Thiene, considering it as roughly contemporary with Palazzo Porto. See also PALLUCCHINI, 1959, and BARBIERI, 1964.

[7] VASARI, 1568, vol. 7, p. 393.

[8] Inigo Jones owned a copy of the Venetian edition of 1601 of the *Quattro Libri*. It is now in Worcester College of Oxford University. For the transcription of Inigo Jones's notes on Palazzo Porto I wish to thank the librarian, R. A. Sayce of Oxford. A facsimile edition of Jones's "Palladio" has now been published.

[9] The catalogue of the R.I.B.A. collection is to be published shortly. The collection consists partly of the drawings that Inigo Jones acquired in Italy and partly of the drawings that Lord Burlington discovered in Villa Barbaro at Maser.

[10] FRÉART DE CHAMBRAY, 1650. The phenomenon of Palladianism in France is treated by HAUTECOEUR, 1952, p. 26, and by BLUNT, 1968.

[11] CAMPBELL, 1715 (-1727). In the first volume there is a plan by Campbell for a palace for the Earl of Islay that has remarkable similarities with Palazzo Porto.

[12] LEONI, 1715, pls. V-VII. See WITTKOWER, 1970.

[13] MUTTONI, 1744, vol. V, pls. V-VII. Muttoni's comment is in the first volume.

[14] TEMANZA, 1762, p. VIII.

[15] BERTOTTI SCAMOZZI, 1761, p. 117 and pl. XXXVI.

[16] BERTOTTI SCAMOZZI, 1776, vol. I, pls. VI-IX.

[17] ARNALDI ET AL., 1779, pt. II, pp. 82 ff.

[18] For Vicentine Neoclassicism we now have a study in depth: BARBIERI, 1972.

[19] MAGRINI, 1845, p. 45.

[20] PULLÉ, 1847.

[21] Cf. the bibliography. A quite thorough treatment of Palazzo Porto is in PÉE, 1939, pp. 58 ff.; BARBIERI-CEVESE-MAGAGNATO, 1956; PANE, 1961, pp. 159 ff.; and ZORZI, 1965, pp. 187 ff.

[22] Still fundamental for the concept of proportions in Palladio is WITTKOWER, 1952, pp. 69 ff., and successive editions (1964). "As the proportions of voices are harmony for our ears, so those of measurements are harmony for our eyes," Palladio himself wrote in a letter (see MAGRINI, 1845, Appendix, p. 12).

[23] BERTOTTI SCAMOZZI, 1776, vol. I: "In fact Palladio says that these rooms are of a height corresponding to the last of the three modes of the heights of vaults prescribed by him, and would be a proportional harmonic mean. Thus they would have to be about 24 feet high, when actually they are only 20 feet and 3 inches... I would not be able to guess how the numerous alterations in the measurements between the designs published by Palladio and the construction of the work that was built came about."

[24] BRANDI, 1960, II, p. 10.

[25] TAFURI, 1969, p. 6.

[26] BENTMANN-MÜLLER, 1970, p. 10. The authors deal principally with the villas of the Veneto, but their analyses also apply to municipal and civil architecture.

[27] See pls. 30 and 31 in ZORZI, 1965. Palladio as an active and passive phenomenon in the social context of his time is a subject that is yet to be studied.

[28] TAFURI (II), 1969, XI.

d) - G<small>IAMBATTISTA</small> T<small>IEPOLO</small>: panel with dove and quiver
(fresco on the vault of the study)

e) - GIAMBATTISTA TIEPOLO: panel with dove (fresco on the vault of the study)

f) - GIAMBATTISTA TIEPOLO: panel with chariot in the clouds (fresco on the vault of the study)

V

THE SURVIVING INTERIOR DECORATIONS
OF THE SIXTEENTH AND EIGHTEENTH CENTURIES

In the Correr manuscript Palladio wrote that on the ground floor of the palace there were "very beautiful paintings by Brusasorzi of Verona and marvelous stuccoes by Ridolfi." The works of the two artists have been preserved in the two rooms at the left of the entrance by the court.

Let us begin in the study, which is situated off the gallery. The four walls are completed on top by a frieze in which we find four groups, each with two reclining figures in high relief (figs. 61 and 62). The figures — some nude, some lightly clothed — probably represent river gods. Behind them we see reeds, and on either side palmettes in monochrome. Similar paired figures appear on the cornice of the Sala dei Principi in Palazzo Thiene, the work of Alessandro Vittoria.[1] Ridolfi, who worked there with Vittoria, reproduced them in the room of Palazzo Porto, but smaller in scale and in a more primitive form. Above there is a cornice with palmettes from which springs a barrel vault, richly ornamented with stuccoes, that contains three panels, two rectangular and one, in the center, hexagonal (figs. 50 and 51). The central figure is framed by a garland, the two laterals by the Vitruvian scroll motif. Between the panels are rectangular and square medallions, as well as triangular and rectangular sections decorated with figures, grotesques, and bunches of grapes. The whole decoration seems quite complex and a little confused. We can take in at a glance the two long friezes with female figures and putti that adorn the lower limits of the barrel vault on both sides, but it is difficult to comprehend their iconographic significance (figs. 55-63). The putti seem to want to push the female figures toward the center, where two embracing women represent the central point. Similar friezes are found in Roman sarcophagi, for example, in the Medea sarcophagus in the National Museum of Rome, which Falconetto had previously used for the decoration of his Odeo Cornaro at Padua.[2] Ridolfi, as Falconetto's son-in-law, would obviously in 1535 have inherited some of his drawings, among which were several taken from Roman monuments.[3] But apart from any such inspiration, the use of motifs from Roman sarcophagi was customary for the decoration of ceilings. Also, the figures in bas-relief, especially the women hovering in the air, the so-called Victories, with richly convoluted fluttering draperies (figs. 66-69), might have been derived from sarcophagus reliefs. Such figures also appear in Palazzo Thiene. The bunches of grapes and the grotesques are designed skillfully and executed accurately. Since the bands on the sides opposite one another correspond exactly, it is legitimate to claim that they were executed with the

XXI - Ottavio Bertotti Scamozzi, *Front elevation of Palazzo da Porto Festa*. From *Le Fabbriche e i Disegni di Andrea Palladio*, Vicenza, I, 1776, pl. VII

aid of a mold (figs. 57 and 58).

The entire decoration, of course, imitates the ancient ceilings rediscovered in the Golden House of Nero by the artists of the Renaissance who, like Raphael and Giovanni da Udine, brought them back to high favor in Rome. Decorations such as those in Villa Madama consist of stuccoes and paintings that we also find in the Odeo Cornaro and Palazzo Thiene. Ridolfi's decorations in Palazzo Porto give special emphasis to the stuccoes, while the pictorial decoration remains circumscribed between panels. It is interesting to observe the absence of those scrolls that Vittoria introduced in Palazzo Thiene in Vicenza and in the Scala d'Oro of Palazzo Ducale in Venice. Those scrolls that are derived from similar motifs in Mantua and Fontainebleau were in that period the most modern decorative element in the Ve-

neto,[4] anticipating the Baroque, while the inspiration for the decoration of Palazzo Porto came from the past. On the other hand, we know how different Ridolfi's attitude was in Palazzo Chiericati, where it is evident that the inspiration came from the Fontainebleau scrolls.[5] Perhaps in Palazzo Porto he had recourse to simpler, less costly forms and had less expert assistants. It does seem, however, that he had not only taken the decoration of Palazzo Thiene as a model, but also that he made use of Vittoria's first work in Vicenza, the barrel vault decorated with stuccoes in Palazzo Bissari Arnaldi, dated about 1547. There we find the same complex system of panels and friezes, highly varied in form, and an even greater richness of detail in the figures and friezes, which Vittoria carried out with greater inventiveness and more refined elegance.[6]

XXII - Ottavio Bertotti Scamozzi, *Section of Palazzo da Porto Festa*. From *Le Fabbriche e i Disegni di Andrea Palladio*, Vicenza, I, 1776, pl. IX

It is not known what the three panels were like before Tiepolo frescoed them during the settecento with open skies in which the few motifs represented seem to allude to pigeon-hunting (figs. 52-53, and *d-e*). A chariot among the clouds (figs. 54 and *f*) is a frequently recurring motif in Tiepolo's skies, for example, in Villa Valmarana ai Nani. The painter understood intuitively and correctly that with stucco decorations so crowded with details, it was necessary that the painting be calm and airy to keep the barrel vault from weighing down too heavily on the small space below. And this is a splendid testimonial of how it was still possible in the eighteenth century to adapt to the taste of the Palladian era.

The adjacent room, which measures 7 x 7 meters, contains Brusasorzi's vault painting of *The Fall of the Giants* (figs. 45-49 and *b-c*). The ribbed groin vault is conceived as the vault of heaven. In the center is Zeus enthroned, expelling the giants from the sky. The giants attempt to defend themselves, but their defeat is inevitable.

Magrini has already indicated the way in which the fresco must be read.[7] We begin with a figure more like a Roman soldier than a giant who is trying to protect himself with his shield from the anger of the god (fig. 45). At his right the nude figures lifting stones to hurl at Zeus display heroic strength, especially the nude man helping a young warrior to lift up a huge stone (fig. 46). In the following segment, to the right, the desperate giants fall, while a pair of monkeys look on (fig. 47). Further to the right in the fourth segment, the giants, whose features are

XXIII - GIULIO PULLÉ, *Façade of Palazzo da Porto Festa*. From *Album di Gemme Architettoniche*,
Venice, 1847; lithograph by Marco Moro

scarcely human, are definitively beaten (fig. 48).

Notwithstanding the numerous figures and the drama of the scene, the vault does not give the impression of a confused piling up of bodies. Each of the four segments contains a dominant figure or groups of figures through which a certain equilibrium in the dynamic conflict is established. The many local colors, among which are Mannerist yellow, orange, violet, and musty green, are all balanced by the predominating flesh tones, so that the color appears harmoniously varied. Several figures are of real beauty, among them the bearded man mentioned above who recalls Titian's *John the Baptist* in the Academy in Venice, even though the treatment of the anatomy is rather uncertain. The monstrous giants are not grotesques,

but rather tragic in expression and attitude.

Brusasorzi, like Ridolfi, came from Verona.[8] Vasari wrote of him: "He is a well-trained and worthy artist, since in addition to painting he is a first-rate musician, one of the best in that most noble philharmonic academy of Verona."[9] Vasari further informed us that Brusasorzi was called to Mantua by Cardinal Ercole Gonzaga, along with other artists from Verona, to work on the Duomo. In the Palazzo del Te, Brusasorzi naturally saw the Fall of the Giants by Giulio Romano and could not avoid being influenced by it. He is thus a part of the Mannerist current that had its center — I go back to Pallucchini's acute definition — at Mantua. Nevertheless, in Palazzo Porto the artist treated the theme in an original manner, both in the composition and in the color. Only the celestial vault and the columnar baldacchino follow Giulio's model.

The year of the execution of the fresco is unknown, but if the date was before 1560 it would constitute the first representation in the Veneto of this important theme, since Battista Franco's *Fall of the Giants* in the Villa Foscari at Malcontenta is dated 1561. Comparing the three versions, we can say that the harsh and intense vision of Giulio Romano contrasts with the more tranquil and detached vision of Brusasorzi, while Battista Franco at Malcontenta reveals a spiritual position not substantially different from that of Michelangelo.

The Fall of the Giants in Palazzo Porto was long attributed to Fasolo. That error is due to Muttoni, who stated that G. B. Fasolo painted the fresco when he was twenty-one, in 1551.[10] Today Palladio's statements on the authorship are accepted. The attribution to Brusasorzi is also confirmed by a comparison with his securely attributed works, for example, the frescoes of Santa Maria in Organo in Verona.[11]

The walls of the room of the Giants today are bare. Arnaldi, who described in laudatory terms *The Fall of the Giants*, added: "Also to be seen on the walls of that place are paintings in chiaroscuro of various illustrious men of that most excellent family by the celebrated brush of Tiepoletto, and of Colonna, which make a fine accompaniment for the Giants."[12] Six portraits of members of the Porto family were taken from the walls of this room around 1900 and found their way to a Berlin collection. In 1929 they were acquired by a Swedish collector and finally they passed into the hands of a London dealer. In 1967 they were exhibited in the Leeds Gallery in Yorkshire.[13]

The portraits (figs. 74-79) are in bronze-colored monochrome about 270 centimeters high. The figures are life size. Each fresco represents an important member of the family in a particular historical situation that is explained by a Latin inscription, for example: "Jacopo Porto, Count and Cavalier, famous for his moral integrity, culture, and wisdom, was made Prefect of Vicenza in 1022 by Henry II, King and Emperor." There we see the Cavalier Jacopo bowing before the emperor with two river gods at their feet. Palladio's Basilica in the background indicates the location of the ceremony (fig. 79). In another fresco General Ippolito Porto appears before the emperor as he consigns to him the Prince of Saxony, who had been taken prisoner at Mühlberg: "After Ippolito Porto, Count and Cavalier, had conquered and made prisoner Prince John of Saxony, he received the highest honors from the Emperor Charles V. He died while fighting the Turks at Corcira" (fig. 76). A third fresco celebrates Gerolamo da Porto for his participation in the war against the League of Cambrai (fig. 77). He is probably the father of Iseppo da Porto; however, neither Iseppo nor his sons appear in the portraits.

In each of the six frescoes the light falls in a different manner. Moreover, they form three pairs with harmonizing backgrounds, allowing us to place them with some sense of security in the room. Standing in the room with our backs to the windows, we would have seen at the left Donato and Francesco Porto in a columnar atrium hung with draperies. On the right wall there would have been Gerolamo and Ippolito Porto in front of undefined architecture, and on the back wall on either side of the door would have been Jacopo and Gian Battista Porto in an open landscape. The subjects have a heroic scale that is not often found in the work of the Tiepolos. Along with the historical or allegorical figures in the entourage, they form groups of remarkable expressive force. The monochromatic color gives these portraits an ideal monumentality that distinguishes them from historical genre of the nineteenth century. Arnaldi is right when he proposes a close relationship of these painted bronzes and Brusasorzi's ceiling fresco. The clear tonalities of Giambattista Tiepolo's historical painting as we see it in Palazzo Labia would have been difficult to place under the sixteenth-century vault. As painted sculpture the portraits harmonize well with the cinquecento tradition. Since Veronese executed painted sculpture for the painted niches of his architectural decorations in Villa Barbaro at Maser, we might imagine that the six Porto portraits were also part of a painted architectonic complex with columns and niches, a motif that came from Roman wall painting.

It is not easy to establish the precise dating of the six portraits, which are unique in the production of the Tiepolos. Muttoni, who described the interior of the palace in 1740, made no comment. However, we do know that the frescoes of Villa Valmarana near Vicenza were executed in 1757. Since Agamemnon in the Room of Homer and several warriors in those frescoes have characteristics similar to these representatives of the Porto family with their exceptional stature, severe faces, and flowing beards, one could say that the painted bronzes in Palazzo Porto were executed contemporaneously with the frescoes of the villa. Also, the paintings in the panels would have been done at about the same time, around 1757. The portraits are today assigned to Giandomenico Tiepolo, while the participation of Colonna is probable in the architectonic details.[14]

The small corridor (measuring scarcely 2.5 x 1.75 meters) that leads from the room we discussed to the room facing the street is decorated on the four walls, around the four doors, and on the vault with frescoes that are of the same period and that appear to be very much restored. On the side of each door there is a candelabrum. Above, there is a painted niche with volutes and a Chinese vase. On the sides of each niche there is a Pan and a nymph elegantly holding a piece of drapery (figs. 80-83). Similar decoration appears in the guest quarters of Villa Valmarana, in the room with the painted stairway. The artist active in Palazzo Porto must have been Colonna, who, as Arnaldi reports, made fresco decorations that are still to be seen in Palazzo Porto Breganze in Contra' Porti — decorations that, however, have no convincing stylistic relationship to the Palazzo Porto decorations.

On the ceiling of the room facing Contra' Porti there are still to be found remains of a fresco that was executed at the same time as the portraits (figs. 72 and 73). The fresco shows, enthroned in the clouds, a member of the Porto family to whom Fame hands a crown of laurel. At his feet sits Cronus, a symbol of earthly transience now overcome.[15] The fresco, transferred to canvas, is now, along with the bozzetto (fig. 70), in the United States in the Seattle Museum (fig. 71).[16] The transferred fresco was restored in a not-altogether-convincing manner. The fresco is unanimously held to be an original work of G. B. Tiepolo, but neither Muttoni nor Arnaldi mentioned it. In the *Gemme Architettoniche* by Zanetti and Marco Moro of 1842 we read: "Balante, Cavalier Liberi, Fasolo, Tiepoletto, and Colonna worked on the paintings commissioned by N. Porti."[17] We cannot, of course, determine whether Zanetti mentioned the name of Tiepolo on the basis of Arnaldi's description of the portraits, or whether he was referring to the ceiling fresco.

The decorations of the ceiling of Villa Cordellina Lombardi at Montecchio Maggiore seem to be near those of Palazzo Porto in subject matter. Both represent an allegory of Fame and have the same open sky with passing clouds and a few figures. However, in the Villa Cordellina the painting is airier, while in Palazzo Porto the representation seems heavier, since the figures of Porto and Cronus constitute a compact mass. From a letter by Tiepolo to Algarotti of 26 October 1743 we learn that the fresco at Montecchio Maggiore was then in the course of execution.[18] Was the fresco in Palazzo Porto executed contemporaneously during Tiepolo's visit of 1743 in Vicenza, or was it started during the later visit of 1757 when the Tiepolos were working in Villa Valmarana and in the other rooms of Palazzo Porto? The answer is up to the experts since I have not seen the original now in Seattle. The same holds for the quality of the fresco, which in any case cannot be numbered among the most significant works of the master.

Three frescoes over the doors in the same room were rediscovered during the restoration of 1954. They are in *grisaille* and consist of volutes and masks. Probably they come from the same studio as the decorations in the small corridor between the main rooms.

The decorations still existing in Palazzo Porto, along with several paintings that belonged to it, now dispersed in Italy, England, and America, give the impression of works of art uprooted from an admirably unified whole. In the era of Palladio and of Veronese and in that of Tiepolo, the ensemble of these works represented a magnificent conception of design, color, and light. To the simple and severe dignity of the exterior with its chiaroscuro was juxtaposed the splendor of the shapes and the colors of the interior.

NOTES TO CHAPTER V

[1] MAGAGNATO, 1966, figs. 65 ff.

[2] On the stuccoes and the frescoes of the Odeo Cornaro, which are of fundamental importance for the decorations of the Venetian houses, see WOLTERS, 1963, and SCHWEIKHART, 1968/1, particularly p. 42 where the sarcophagus of Medea is discussed.

[3] ZORZI, 1959, p. 38.

[4] On the decorative motifs in the circle of Alessandro Vittoria see MAGAGNATO, 1966, pp. 45 ff. and WOLTERS, in which the decorations of Palazzo Porto are also taken into consideration on p. 44 (as the work of Ridolfi).

[5] On the ceiling of the second room on the left, cf. BARBIERI, 1962, I, fig. 8.

[6] On the ceiling of Casa Arnaldi-Bissari, see WOLTERS, 1968, p. 32, fig. 36.

[7] MAGRINI, 1851, pp. 58 ff. Like almost all scholars Magrini attributed the Fall of the Giants to Fasolo and expressed an unfavorable opinion of it.

[8] Cf. MAGAGNATO, 1968, X, pp. 170 ff.

[9] In VASARI's life of Sanmicheli, 1568, vol. 6, p. 260.

[10] MUTTONI, 1740, vol. I, pp. 8 ff.

[11] While in the *Guida di Vicenza*, Vicenza, 1956, p. 114, and in ZORZI, 1965, p. 195, the Fall of the Giants was still attributed to Fasolo, PALLUCCHINI, 1960, had already raised doubts about the traditional attribution. Successive scholars saw in it a work by Domenico Rizzo, called Brusasorzi: CROSATO, 1962, p. 42; PALLUCCHINI, 1968, X, p. 227; and MAGAGNATO, 1968, X, p. 178.

[12] ARNALDI ET AL., 1779, p. 86.

[13] Cf. the catalogue *Tiepolo Frescoes from the Palazzo Porto*, *Vicenza*, Leeds, 1967. For the photographs of the six portraits, I am indebted to the Hallsborough Gallery of London.

[14] MORASSI, London, 1962, p. 48, dated the portraits to the years 1755-60, which he records as being still in Stockholm, and saw the collaboration of Giandomenico in them. See VIGNI, 1943, p. 14, and MARIUZ, 1971, p. 122, for the attribution of the portraits to Giandomenico.

[15] MORASSI, 1962, p. 48, dated the Apotheosis of Orazio Porto to 1755-60. Orazio Porto was cited by Bertotti Scamozzi as the owner of the palace. The problem of whether the Apotheosis really refers to Orazio or to another Porto remains unresolved.

[16] The fresco measures 5.08 x 3.03 meters. Its history is described in the catalogue *European Paintings and Sculpture from the Samuel Kress Collection*, Seattle Art Museum, 1954, p. 78. In regard to the remains of the fresco (detached) from Palazzo Porto it states: "These traces have since been restored by Pellicioli, who also has done the recent restoration of Leonardo's Last Supper in Milan." The Seattle Museum also possesses the water-color sketch of the fresco, which was acquired in 1961.

[17] PULLÉ, 1847.

[18] MORASSI, 1943, pp. 25 ff.

BIBLIOGRAPHY

1545 S. SERLIO, *Il Secondo Libro di Perspectiva*, Paris.

1556 D. BARBARO, *I Dieci Libri dell'Architettura di M. Vitruvio*, Venice.

1565 L. B. ALBERTI, *L'Architettura*, Venice.

1568 G. VASARI, *Le vite de' più eccellenti pittori scultori e architettori*, Florence [ed. Club del Libro, Milan, 1964.]

1570 A. PALLADIO, *I Quattro Libri dell'Architettura*, Venice.

1591 G. MARZARI, *Historia di Vicenza*, Venice.

1650 J. FRÉART DE CHAMBRAY, *Les quatre Livres de l'Architecture d'André Palladio*, Paris.

1715 C. CAMPBELL, *Vitruvius Britannicus or the British Architecht*, London.

1715 G. LEONI, *The Architecture of Andrea Palladio in Four Books*, London.

1738 I. WARE, *The Four Books of Andrea Palladio's Architecture*, London.

1740 [F. MUTTONI], *Architettura di Andrea Palladio Vicentino di nuovo ristampata... con le osservazioni dell'architetto N. N.*, Venice.

1761 [O. BERTOTTI SCAMOZZI], *Il Forestiere Istruito Delle Cose più rare di Architettura. Dialogo di Ottavio Bertotti Scamozzi dedicato al Nob. Marchese Mario Capra*, Vicenza.

1762 T. TEMANZA, *Vita di Andrea Palladio Vicentino*, Venice.

1776 J. T. FACCIOLI, *Museum Lapidarium Vicentinum*, Vicenza.

1776-1783 O. BERTOTTI SCAMOZZI, *Le Fabbriche e i Disegni di Andrea Palladio*, Vicenza.

1779 [E. ARNALDI ET AL.], *Descrizione delle Architettura, Pitture, e Sculture di Vicenza con alcune osservazioni. Parte Seconda. Degli edifici pubblici, e privati*, Vicenza.

1791 A. MUCCI, *I Quattro Libri dell'Architettura di Andrea Palladio*, Siena.

1822 G. B. BERTI, *Guida per Vicenza ossia memorie storico-critico-descrittive di questa Regia Città*, Vicenza.

1845 A. MAGRINI, *Dell'architettura in Vicenza. Discorso*, Padua.

1845 A. MAGRINI, *Memorie intorno la vita e le opere di Andrea Palladio*, Padua.

1847 G. PULLÉ, *Album di gemme architettoniche*, Vicenza.

1851 A. MAGRINI, *Cenni storico-critici sulla vita e sulle opere di Giovanni Antonio Fasolo*, Venice.

1856 F. TRISSINO, *Vita di Stefano Madonetta Pittore Vicentino*, Vicenza.

1887 D. S. RUMOR, *Il castello di Santa Maria in Thiene, I Porto - I Colleoni*, Vicenza.

1892 B. MORSOLIN, "Medaglia in onore di Giuseppe da Porto," in *Rivista Italiana di Numismatica*.

1939 R. PALLUCCHINI, *Paolo Veronese*, exhibition catalogue, Venice.

1939 H. PÉE, *Die Palastbauten des Andrea Palladio*, Würzburg.

1940 A. VENTURI, *Storia dell'arte italiana. Architettura del Cinquecento*, vol. XI, pt. III, Milan.

1943 A. M. DALLA POZZA, *Palladio*, Vicenza.

1943 A. MORASSI, *Tiepolo*, Bergamo.

1943 VIGNI, "Notizie su G. B. e G. D. Tiepolo," in *Emporium*.

1951 G. ZORZI, "Alessandro Vittoria a Vicenza e lo scultore Lorenzo Rubini," in *Arte Veneta*.

1952 R. CEVESE, *I Palazzi dei Thiene*, Vicenza.

1952 L. HAUTECOEUR, *L'Architecture Classique en France*, Paris.

1952 R. WITTKOWER, *Architectural Principles in the Age of Humanism*, London (Italian ed., 1964).

1954 L. MAGAGNATO, *Teatri del Cinquecento*, Venice.

1954 G. ZORZI, "Progetti giovanili di Andrea Palladio per palazzi e case in Venezia e in Terraferma," in *Palladio*.
G. ZORZI, *European Painting and Sculpture from the Samuel H. Kress Collection*, Seattle Art Museum, p. 78.

1956 F. BARBIERI - R. CEVESE - L. MAGAGNATO, *Guida di Vicenza*, Vicenza.

1959 G. MASSON, *Italienische Villen und Paläste*, Munich-Zürich.

1959 R. PALLUCCHINI, "Andrea Palladio e Giulio Romano," in *Bollettino del Centro Internazionale di Studi di Architettura A. Palladio*, I, Vicenza.

1959 G. ZORZI, *I Disegni delle Antichità di Andrea Palladio*, Venice.

1960 C. BRANDI, "Perché Palladio non fu neoclassico," in *Bollettino del Centro Internazionale di Studi di Architettura A. Palladio*, II, Vicenza.

1960 F. CESSI, *Alessandro Vittoria medaglista (1525-1608)*, Trent.

1960 R. PALLUCCHINI, *Palladio, Veronese e Vittoria a Maser*, Milan.

1961 R. PANE, *Andrea Palladio*, Turin.

1961 G. ZORZI, "Giovanni Antonio Fasolo," in *Arte Lombarda*.

1962 F. BARBIERI, *Il Museo Civico di Vicenza*, Venice.

1962 L. CROSATO, *Gli affreschi nelle ville venete del Cinquecento*, Treviso.

1962   A. MORASSI, *A Complete Catalogue of the Painting of G. B. Tiepolo*, London.

1963   W. WOLTERS, "Tiziano Minio als Stukator in Odeo Cornaro zu Padua," in *Pantheon*, XXI.

1964   F. BARBIERI, "Palladio e il Manierismo," in *Bollettino del Centro Internazionale di Studi di Architettura A. Palladio*, VI, Vicenza.

1965   E. FORSSMAN, *Palladios Lehrgebäude. Studien Über den Zusammenhang von Architektur und Architekturtheorie bei Andrea Palladio*, Stockholm.

1965   G. ZORZI, *Le opere pubbliche e i palazzi privati di Andrea Palladio*, Venice.

1966   J. S. ACKERMAN, *Palladio*, London, pp. 103 ff.

1966   R. CEVESE, "Il palazzo da Porto Festa," in *Vicenza Economica*, XXI.

1966   L. MAGAGNATO, *Palazzo Thiene*, Vicenza.

1966   L. PUPPI, *Palladio*, Florence.

1967   *Tiepolo Frescoes from the Palazzo Porto, Vicenza*. Catalogue of the Temple Newsam House Museum, Leeds.

1967   N. IVANOFF, *Palladio*, Milan.

1968   F. BARBIERI, *La Basilica Palladiana*, Vicenza.

1968   A. BLUNT, "Palladio in Francia," in *Bollettino del Centro Internazionale di Studi di Architettura A. Palladio*, X, Vicenza.

1968   L. MAGAGNATO, "I collaboratori veronesi di Andrea Palladio," in *Bollettino del Centro Internazionale di Studi di Architettura A. Palladio*, X, Vicenza.

1968   R. PALLUCCHINI, "Giambattista Zelotti e Giovanni Antonio Fasolo," in *Bollettino del Centro Internazionale di Studi di Architettura A. Palladio*, X, Vicenza.

1968   G. PIOVENE, R. MARINI, *L'opera completa del Veronese*, Milan.

1968   G. SCHWEIKHART, "Studien zum Werke des Giovanni Maria," in *Bollettino del Museo Civico di Padova*.

1968   C. SEMENZATO, *La Rotonda*, Vicenza.

1968   R. WITTKOWER, "Il balaustro rinascimentale e il Palladio," in *Bollettino del Centro Internazionale di Studi di Architettura A. Palladio*, X, Vicenza.

1968   W. WOLTERS, *Plastiche Deckendekorationen des Cinquecento in Venedig und im Veneto*, Berlin.

1968   G. ZORZI, *Le ville e i teatri di Andrea Palladio*, Venice.

1969   W. PRINZ, "La 'sala di quattro colonne' nell'opera di Palladio," in *Bollettino del Centro Internazionale di Studi di Architettura A. Palladio*, XI, Vicenza.

1969   M. TAFURI, *Jacopo Sansovino e l'architettura del Cinquecento a Venezia*, Padua.

1969   M. TAFURI (II), "Committenza e tipologia nelle ville palladiane," in *Bollettino del Centro Internazionale di Studi di Architettura A. Palladio*, XI, Vicenza.

1969   S. WILINSKI, "La serliana," in *Bollettino del Centro Internazionale di Studi di Architettura A. Palladio*, XI, Vicenza.

1970   F. BARBIERI, "Palladio in Villa negli anni quaranta: da Lonedo a Bagnolo," in *Arte Veneta*, XXIV.

1970   R. BENTMANN - M. MÜLLER, *Die Villa als Herrschaftsarchitektur. Versuch einer kunst- und sozialgeschichtlichen Analyse*, Frankfurt.

1970   R. WITTKOWER, "Le edizioni inglesi del Palladio," in *Bollettino del Centro Internazionale di Studi di Architettura A. Palladio*, XII, Vicenza.

1971   A. MARIUZ, *Giandomenico Tiepolo*, Venice.

1971   B. RUPPRECHT, "Palladios Projekt für den Palazzo Iseppo Porto in Vicenza," in *Mitteilungen des kunsthistorischen Instituts in Florenz*, XV.

1972   F. BARBIERI, *Illuministi e neoclassici a Vicenza*, Vicenza.

INDEX OF NAMES AND PLACES

Proper names are in capitals; place names are in italics.

ALBERTI, LEONBATTISTA, 26, 33
ALGAROTTI, FRANCESCO, 67
ARNALDI, ENEA, 40, 41, 52, 66, 67

BALANTE DA THIENE, 40, 41, 66
BARBARO, DANIELE, 41, 46
BARBIERI, FRANCO, 33, 41, 60, 67
BARRERA, CARLO, 52
BECCANUVOLI, LUCREZIO, 13, 20
BENTMANN, REINHARD, 60
BERTI, G. B., 41
BERTOTTI SCAMOZZI, OTTAVIO, 8, 46, 50, 53, 60
BIEGO, LUIGI, 19
BLUNT, ANTHONY, 60
Bologna, 13
BRAMANTE, DONATO, 23, 25, 27, 43
BRANDI, CESARE, 60
BRUSASORZI, DOMENICO, 28, 61, 63, 64, 65
BURLINGTON, RICHARD (LORD), 48, 60
CALDERARI, OTTONE, 35, 52
CAMPBELL, COLIN, 48, 60
CATANEO, PIETRO, 33
CESSI, FRANCESCO, 21
CEVESE, RENATO, 21, 60
CHARLES V, 13, 65
CIAN, ANTONIO, 41
CODUCCI, MAURO, 44
COLLEONI - PORTO, GENTILE, 19
COLLEONI - PORTO, ORAZIO GUARDINO, 19, 39, 41
Corfù, 13
CROSATO, LUCIANA, 67

DA PORTO, ADRIANO, 13, 14, 19, 31
DA PORTO, DEIDAMIA, 14
DA PORTO, GEROLAMO, 13, 65
DA PORTO, GIUSEPPE, 40
DA PORTO, IPPOLITO, 13, 65
DA PORTO, IRENE, 40
DA PORTO, ISEPPO, 13, 14, 19, 23, 36, 48, 65
DA PORTO, LEONIDA, 13, 14, 19, 31, 36
DA PORTO, MADDALENA ANGARANA, 40
DA PORTO, PORZIA, 13

DA SCHIO, 20
DIEDO, ANTONIO, 39

FACCIOLI, J. T., 14, 21
FALCONETTO, GIOVANNI MARIA, 23, 27, 43, 61
Fano, 46
FASOLO, GIOVANNI BATTISTA, 65, 66
FESTA, ITALO, 19
FESTA, MARIA COSTANZA CANERA DI SALASCO, 19
Fontainebleau, 62
FOSSATI, GIORGIO, 48
FRANCO, BATTISTA, 65
Fratta Polesine
    Villa Badoer, 41
FRÉART DE CHAMBRAY, J., 48, 60

GIACOMETTI, GIUSEPPE, 40
GIOVANNI DA UDINE, 62
GIULIO ROMANO, 41, 64
Greenwich, 46

HAUTECOEUR, LOUIS, 60
HENRY II, 65
HENRY IV, 20

JONES, INIGO, 46, 60

Leeds, 65, 67
LEONI, GIACOMO, 48
LEVAU, LOUIS, 48
LIBERI, PIETRO, 40, 41, 66
London, 23, 46, 48

MAGAGNATO, LICISCO, 20, 41, 60, 67
MAGANZA, ALESSANDRO, 19
MAGRINI, ANTONIO, 14, 39, 52, 63, 67
MALASPINA, ANNA, 14
Malcontenta
    Villa Foscari, 41, 65
Mantua, 62, 64
Marano, 14
MARINI, REMIGIO, 20
MARIUZ, ADRIANO, 67
MARX, KARL, 60
MARZARI, G., 20

Maser
    Villa Barbaro, 41, 60, 66
MENGOZZI-COLONNA, GEROLAMO, 65, 66
MICHELANGELO, 38, 58
Molina, 14, 19, 21
Montecchio Maggiore
    Villa Cordellina Lombardi, 67
MORASSI, ANTONIO, 67
MORO, MARCO, 44, 52, 66
MORSOLIN, BERNARDO, 21
MUCCI, ALESSANDRO, 50
MÜLLER, MICHAEL, 60

Oxford
    Worcester College, 60

Padua, 24
PALLUCCHINI, RODOLFO, 20, 60, 64, 67
PAVAN, LUIGI, 40
PÉE, HERBERT, 60
PELLICCIOLI, 67
PERUZZI, BALDASSARE, 41
PIAZZETTA, GIAMBATTISTA, 40, 41
PIOVENE, ANTONIO, 52
PIOVENE, GUIDO, 20
Possagno, 39
PRINZ, WOLFRAM, 41
PULLÉ, GIULIO, 60, 67

Quinto Vicentino, 14

RAPHAEL, 25, 27, 43, 62
RIDOLFI, BARTOLOMEO, 28, 41, 61, 64, 67
Rome, 23, 43, 46
    Domus aurea, 46, 62
    Palazzo Massimo alle Colonne, 44
    Pantheon, 39
    Villa Madama, 26
RONCALLI, CATERINA, 39
RUBINI, LORENZO, 36, 41
RUMOR, SEBASTIANO, 20, 40

S. Sofia (Verona), 29
SANGALLO, ANTONIO, 43
SANMARTIN, MANLIO, 21, 41

SANMICHELI, MICHELE, 23, 24, 27, 41, 43, 44
SANSOVINO, JACOPO, 44, 58
SAYCE, R. A., 60
SCAMOZZI, GIANDOMENICO, 19
SCAMOZZI, VINCENZO, 46
SCHWEIKHART, GUNTER, 67
Seattle, 66, 67
SELVA, GIOVANNI ANTONIO, 39
SEMENZATO, CAMILLO, 41
SERLIO, SEBASTIANO, 13, 20, 59

TAFURI, MANFREDO, 60
TEMANZA, TOMMASO, 14, 21, 48
Thiene, 13, 20, 21
THIENE, ATTILIA, 14
THIENE, CLEMENTE, 20
THIENE, GIOVANNI GALEAZZO, 20
THIENE, LIVIA, 13, 14, 23
THIENE, LUCIA, 20
THIENE, MARCO ANTONIO, 13, 21
TIEPOLO, GIAMBATTISTA, 41, 52, 63, 65, 66, 67

TIEPOLO, GIANDOMENICO, 66, 67
TITIAN, 64
TOMASINI, FRANCESCO, 20, 21
TRISSINO, F., 41

Udine
    Palazzo Antonini, 41

VASARI, GIORGIO, 46, 60, 64, 67
Venice
    Convento della Carità, 29, 44
    Museo Correr, 28, 31, 39, 40, 61
VERONESE, PAOLO, 13, 30, 40, 66, 67
Versailles, 48
Vicenza
    Accademia Olimpica, 14
    Basilica, 35
    Church of S. Biagio, 14, 21, 32
    Loggia del Capitanio, 36
    Palazzo Bissari Arnaldi, 62
    Palazzo Civena, 23, 24, 36, 43
    Palazzo Cordellina, 35, 52

    Palazzo Loschi Zileri Dal Verme, 35, 52
    Palazzo Pojana, 33
    Palazzo Porto Barbaran, 36, 52
    Palazzo Porto Breganze, 64
    Palazzo Porto-Colleoni, 13
    Palazzo Thiene, 14, 23, 25, 26, 32, 36, 38, 43, 44, 61, 62
    Palazzo Valmarana, 32
    Villa Rotonda, 38, 39
VITRUVIUS, M. P., 24, 27, 28, 29, 30, 35, 36, 38, 41, 44, 46, 53
VITTORIA, ALESSANDRO, 14, 36, 41, 61, 62

WARE, ISAAC, 48
WILINSKI, STANISLAW, 41
WITTKOWER, RUDOLF, 41, 60
WOLTERS, WOLFGANG, 67

ZANETTI, 66
ZORZI, GIANGIORGIO, 14, 21, 33, 41

ILLUSTRATIONS IN THE TEXT

I   ALESSANDRO VITTORIA (?), *Medal with the portrait of Iseppo da Porto (recto and verso)*

II   PAOLO VERONESE, *Portrait of Iseppo da Porto with his son Adriano.* Florence, Uffizi

III   PAOLO VERONESE, *Portrait of Livia da Porto with daughter.* Baltimore, Walters Art Gallery

IV   UNKNOWN VENETIAN PAINTER OF THE SIXTEENTH CENTURY, *Portrait of Iseppo da Porto.* Thiene, Villa da Porto, now Thiene

V   ANDREA PALLADIO, *First design for the façade of Palazzo da Porto Festa.* London, R.I.B.A., XVII, 12r

VI   ANDREA PALLADIO, *Second design for the façade of Palazzo da Porto Festa.* London, R.I.B.A., XVII, 9r

VII   ANDREA PALLADIO, *Third design for the façade of Palazzo da Porto Festa.* London, R.I.B.A., XVII, 12v

VIII   ANDREA PALLADIO, *First design for the floor plan of Palazzo da Porto Festa.* London, R.I.B.A., XVI, 8

IX   ANDREA PALLADIO, *Second design for the floor plan of Palazzo da Porto Festa.* London, R.I.B.A., XVII, 9v

X   ANDREA PALLADIO, *Design of the front elevation and the courtyard of Palazzo da Porto Festa for the woodcut for the* Quattro Libri. London, R.I.B.A., XVII, 3

XI   ANDREA PALLADIO, *Floor plan and section of Palazzo da Porto Festa.* From *I Quattro Libri dell'Architettura,* Venice, 1570, II, chapter III, p. 8

XII   ANDREA PALLADIO, *Front elevation of Palazzo da Porto Festa.* From *I Quattro Libri dell'Architettura,* Venice, 1570, II, chapter III, p. 9

XIII   ANDREA PALLADIO, *Elevation on the courtyard of Palazzo da Porto Festa.* From *I Quattro Libri dell'Architettura,* Venice, 1570, II, chapter III, p. 10

XIV   ISAAC WARE, *Ground plan and section of Palazzo da Porto Festa.* From *I Quattro Libri dell'Architettura,* London, 1738, I, pl. IV

XV   ISAAC WARE, *Front elevation of Palazzo da Porto Festa.* From *The Four Books of Andrea Palladio's Architecture,* London, 1738, I, pl. V

XVI   FRANCESCO MUTTONI, *Plan of Palazzo da Porto Festa.* From *Architettura di Andrea Palladio Vicentino,* Venice, 1744, V, pl. V

XVII   ALESSANDRO MUCCI, *Front elevation of Palazzo da Porto Festa.* From *I Quattro Libri dell'Architettura di Andrea Palladio,* Siena, 1791, II, p. 13

XVIII   ANDREA PALLADIO, *The House of the Ancient Romans.* From *I Quattro Libri dell'Architettura,* II, chapter VII, p. 34

XIX   FRANCESCO MUTTONI, *Elevation on the courtyard of Palazzo da Porto Festa.* From *Architettura di Andrea Palladio Vicentino,* Venice, 1744, V, pl. VI

XX   GIACOMO LEONI, *Elevation on the courtyard of Palazzo da Porto Festa.* From *The Architecture of A. Palladio in four books,* London, 1721, II, pl. VII

XXI   OTTAVIO BERTOTTI SCAMOZZI, *Front elevation of Palazzo da Porto Festa.* From *Le Fabbriche e i Disegni di Andrea Palladio,* Vicenza, I, 1776, pl. VII

XXII   OTTAVIO BERTOTTI SCAMOZZI, *Section of Palazzo da Porto Festa.* From *Le Fabbriche e i Disegni di Andrea Palladio,* Vicenza, I, 1776, pl. IX

XXIII   GIULIO PULLÉ, *Façade of Palazzo da Porto Festa.* From *Album di Gemme Architettoniche,* Venice, 1847; lithograph by Marco Moro

PLATES

1   Vicenza. Aerial view of the Porto Festa complex with the unfinished east side of the palace (in the photograph at the left of the gothic loggia) facing the courtyard and the hanging garden where the second section of the palace itself would have stood

2   Vicenza. Contra' Porti with the Palazzo da Porto Festa at the rear

3   Vicenza. The gothic Palazzo Porto-Colleoni and the Palazzo da Porto Festa

4   Palazzo da Porto Festa: the entrance façade, seen from the left

5   Palazzo da Porto Festa: the entrance façade seen from the right

6   Palazzo da Porto Festa: left section of the façade

7   Palazzo da Porto Festa: the *piano nobile* and the attic story

8   Palazzo da Porto Festa: the ground-floor windows on the left

9   Palazzo da Porto Festa: the ground-floor windows on the right

10   Palazzo da Porto Festa: the second window from the left on the ground floor

11   Palazzo da Porto Festa: the entrance portal

12-13   Palazzo da Porto Festa: the two windows at the end of the *piano nobile*

14   Palazzo da Porto Festa: the center window of the *piano nobile*

15-16   Palazzo da Porto Festa: two windows of the *piano nobile*

17   Palazzo da Porto Festa: an Ionic order capital and entablature above

18   Palazzo da Porto Festa: two balconies on the *piano nobile*

19   Palazzo da Porto Festa: the base of an Ionic column

20-21-22   Palazzo da Porto Festa: masks above the ground-floor windows

23-24-25   Palazzo da Porto Festa: masks above the ground-floor windows

26   Palazzo da Porto Festa: statue of Iseppo da Porto on the attic story

27   Palazzo da Porto Festa: statue of Leonida da Porto on the attic story

28   Palazzo da Porto Festa: arrangement of the two statues of Iseppo and Leonida da Porto on the attic story

29-30   Palazzo da Porto Festa: the two statues at either end of the attic

31   Palazzo da Porto Festa: view of the atrium from the entrance portal

32   Palazzo da Porto Festa: view of the atrium facing the entrance portal

33   Palazzo da Porto Festa: detail of the atrium

34   Palazzo da Porto Festa: detail of the atrium

35   Palazzo da Porto Festa: detail of the atrium

36   Palazzo da Porto Festa: detail of the atrium

37   Palazzo da Porto Festa: detail of the atrium

38   Palazzo da Porto Festa: detail of the atrium

39   Palazzo da Porto Festa: east side of the courtyard

40   Palazzo da Porto Festa: east side of the courtyard (as carried out in a scale model)

41   Palazzo da Porto Festa: an angle of the courtyard, between the east and the south sides (as carried out in the model)

42   Palazzo da Porto Festa: detail of an angle of the courtyard between the east and the south sides (as carried out in the model)

43   Palazzo da Porto Festa: the courtyard seen from above (as carried out in the model)

44   Palazzo da Porto Festa: view of the upper loggia in the east side of the model

45   DOMENICO BRUSASORZI: *The Fall of the Giants*, detail (vault fresco in the square room on the ground floor)

46-47   DOMENICO BRUSASORZI: *The Fall of the Giants*, details (vault fresco in the square room on the ground floor)

48   DOMENICO BRUSASORZI: *The Fall of the Giants*, detail (vault fresco in the square room on the ground floor)

49   DOMENICO BRUSASORZI: *The Fall of the Giants*, detail of the center of the vault

50   Palazzo da Porto Festa: barrel vault in the study, seen from the west side

51   Palazzo da Porto Festa: barrel vault in the study, seen from the east side

52   GIAMBATTISTA TIEPOLO: panel with dove (fresco on the vault of the study)

53   GIAMBATTISTA TIEPOLO: panel with dove and quiver (fresco on the vault of the study)

54   GIAMBATTISTA TIEPOLO: panel with chariot in clouds (fresco on the vault of the study)

55   BARTOLOMEO RIDOLFI: stuccoes in the vault of the study
56   BARTOLOMEO RIDOLFI: stuccoes in the vault of the study
57   BARTOLOMEO RIDOLFI: stuccoes in the vault of the study
58   BARTOLOMEO RIDOLFI: stuccoes in the vault of the study
59   BARTOLOMEO RIDOLFI: stuccoes in the vault of the study
60   BARTOLOMEO RIDOLFI: stuccoes in the vault of the study
61   BARTOLOMEO RIDOLFI: stucco frieze in the study, detail
62   BARTOLOMEO RIDOLFI: stucco frieze in the study, detail
63   BARTOLOMEO RIDOLFI: stucco frieze in the study, detail
64   BARTOLOMEO RIDOLFI: stucco frieze in the study, detail
65   BARTOLOMEO RIDOLFI: stucco frieze in the study, detail
66   BARTOLOMEO RIDOLFI: stucco frieze in the study, detail
67   BARTOLOMEO RIDOLFI: stucco frieze in the study, detail
68   BARTOLOMEO RIDOLFI: stucco frieze in the study, detail
69   BARTOLOMEO RIDOLFI: stucco frieze in the study, detail
70   GIAMBATTISTA TIEPOLO: bozzetto for the ceiling of the ground-floor salon. Seattle Art Museum
71   GIAMBATTISTA TIEPOLO: fresco formerly on the ceiling of the ground-floor salon. Seattle Art Museum
72   GIAMBATTISTA TIEPOLO: remnant of the detached fresco on the ceiling of the ground-floor salon
73   GIAMBATTISTA TIEPOLO: remnant of the detached fresco on the ceiling of the ground floor salon, detail
74   GIANDOMENICO TIEPOLO: *Francesco da Porto Named General of the Venetian Republic*
75   GIANDOMENICO TIEPOLO: *Donato da Porto Made a Patrician of Venice*
76   GIANDOMENICO TIEPOLO: *Ippolito da Porto Decorated by Charles V*
77   GIANDOMENICO TIEPOLO: *Gerolamo da Porto Named Prefect of Piedmont*
78   GIANDOMENICO TIEPOLO: *Giovanni Battista da Porto Named Commander-in-Chief*
79   GIANDOMENICO TIEPOLO: *Jacopo da Porto Named Governor of Vicenza*
80-81-82-83   Palazzo da Porto Festa: frescoes in the hallway between the room of the Giants and the ground-floor salon
84   Palazzo da Porto Festa: cupola in the southeast corner room of the *piano nobile* with Pompeian motifs; a nineteenth-century fresco
85   Palazzo da Porto Festa: the Neoclassical rotunda on the *piano nobile*
86   Palazzo da Porto Festa: cupola of the Neoclassical rotunda on the *piano nobile*
87   Palazzo da Porto Festa: Neoclassical frieze in the rotunda on the *piano nobile*, detail of Homage to Architecture
88   Palazzo da Porto Festa: Neoclassical frieze in the rotunda on the *piano nobile*, detail of Homage to Sculpture
89   Palazzo da Porto Festa: Neoclassical frieze in the rotunda on the *piano nobile*, detail of probable portraits of Orazio Colleoni-Porto and Caterina Roncalli
90   Palazzo da Porto Festa: Neoclassical frieze in the rotunda on the *piano nobile*, detail of Homage to Painting

COLOR PLATES:

a   Palazzo da Porto Festa: façade seen from the left
b   DOMENICO BRUSASORZI: *The Fall of the Giants*, detail (fresco on the vault of the square room on the ground floor)
c   DOMENICO BRUSASORZI: *The Fall of the Giants*, detail (fresco on the vault of the square room on the ground floor)
d   GIAMBATTISTA TIEPOLO: panel with dove and quiver (fresco on the vault of the study)
e   GIAMBATTISTA TIEPOLO: panel with dove (fresco on the vault of the study)
f   GIAMBATTISTA TIEPOLO: panel with chariot in the clouds (fresco on the vault of the study)

SCALE DRAWINGS

I   Palazzo da Porto Festa: topographical plan of the area

II   Palazzo da Porto Festa: plan of the ground floor

III   Palazzo da Porto Festa: plan of the *piano nobile*

IV   Palazzo da Porto Festa: plan of the attic story

V   Palazzo da Porto Festa: elevation facing the street

VI   Palazzo da Porto Festa: elevation facing the court

VII   Palazzo da Porto Festa: longitudinal section, taken along the central axis

VIII Palazzo da Porto Festa: longitudinal section, taken to the side of the entrance

IX   Palazzo da Porto Festa: details of the elevation facing the street

PLATES

1 - Vicenza. Aerial view of the Porto Festa complex with the unfinished east side of the palace (in the photograph at the left of the gothic loggia) facing the courtyard and the hanging garden where the second section of the palace itself would have stood

2 - Vicenza. Contra' Porti with the Palazzo da Porto Festa at the rear

3 - Vicenza. The gothic Palazzo Porto-Colleoni and the Palazzo da Porto Festa

4 - Palazzo da Porto Festa: the entrance façade, seen from the left

5 - Palazzo da Porto Festa: the entrance façade seen from the right

6 - Palazzo da Porto Festa: left section of the façade

7 - Palazzo da Porto Festa: the *piano nobile* and the attic story

8 - Palazzo da Porto Festa: the ground-floor windows on the left

9 - Palazzo da Porto Festa: the ground-floor windows on the right

10 - Palazzo da Porto Festa: the second window from the left on the ground floor

11 - Palazzo da Porto Festa: the entrance portal

12-13 - Palazzo da Porto Festa: the two windows at the ends of the *piano nobile*

14 - Palazzo da Porto Festa: the center window of the *piano nobile*

15-16 · Palazzo da Porto Festa: two windows of the *piano nobile*

17 - Palazzo da Porto Festa: an Ionic order capital and entablature above

18 - Palazzo da Porto Festa: two balconies on the *piano nobile*

19 - Palazzo da Porto Festa: the base of an Ionic column

20-21-22 - Palazzo da Porto Festa: masks above the ground-floor windows

23-24-25 - Palazzo da Porto Festa: masks above the ground-floor
windows

26 - Palazzo da Porto Festa: statue of Iseppo da Porto on the attic story

27 - Palazzo da Porto Festa: statue of Leonida da Porto on the attic story

28 - Palazzo da Porto Festa: arrangement of the two statues of Iseppo and Leonida da Porto on the attic story

29-30 - Palazzo da Porto Festa: the two statues at either end of the attic

31 - Palazzo da Porto Festa: view of the atrium from the entrance portal

32 - Palazzo da Porto Festa: view of the atrium facing the entrance portal

33 - Palazzo da Porto Festa: detail of the atrium

34 - Palazzo da Porto Festa: detail of the atrium

35 - Palazzo da Porto Festa: detail of the atrium

36 - Palazzo da Porto Festa: detail of the atrium

37 - Palazzo da Porto Festa: detail of the atrium

38 - Palazzo da Porto Festa: detail of the atrium

39 - Palazzo da Porto Festa: east side of the courtyard

40 - Palazzo da Porto Festa: east side of the courtyard (as carried out in a scale model)

41 - Palazzo da Porto Festa: an angle of the courtyard, between the east and the south sides (as carried out in the model)

42 - Palazzo da Porto Festa: detail of an angle of the courtyard between the east and the south sides (as carried out in the model)

43 - Palazzo da Porto Festa: the courtyard seen from above (as carried out in the model)

44 - Palazzo da Porto Festa: view of the upper loggia in the east side of the model

45 - DOMENICO BRUSASORZI: *The Fall of the Giants*, detail (vault fresco in the square room on the ground floor)

46-47 - DOMENICO BRUSASORZI: *The Fall of the Giants,* details (vault fresco in the square room on the ground floor)

48 - Domenico Brusasorzi: *The Fall of the Giants*, detail (vault fresco in the square room on the ground floor)

49 - DOMENICO BRUSASORZI: *The Fall of the Giants*, detail of the center of the vault

50 - Palazzo da Porto Festa: barrel vault in the study, seen from the west side

51 - Palazzo da Porto Festa: barrel vault in the study, seen from the east side

52 - GIAMBATTISTA TIEPOLO: panel with dove (fresco on the vault of the study)

53 - Giambattista Tiepolo: panel with dove and quiver (fresco on the vault of the study)

54 - GIAMBATTISTA TIEPOLO: panel with chariot in clouds (fresco on the vault of the study)

55 - BARTOLOMEO RIDOLFI: stuccoes in the vault of the study

56 - Bartolomeo Ridolfi: stuccoes in the vault of the study

57 - Bartolomeo Ridolfi: stuccoes in the vault of the study

58 - Bartolomeo Ridolfi: stuccoes in the vault of the study

59 - BARTOLOMEO RIDOLFI: stuccoes in the vault of the study

60 - Bartolomeo Ridolfi: stuccoes in the vault of the study

61 - Bartolomeo Ridolfi: stucco frieze in the study, detail

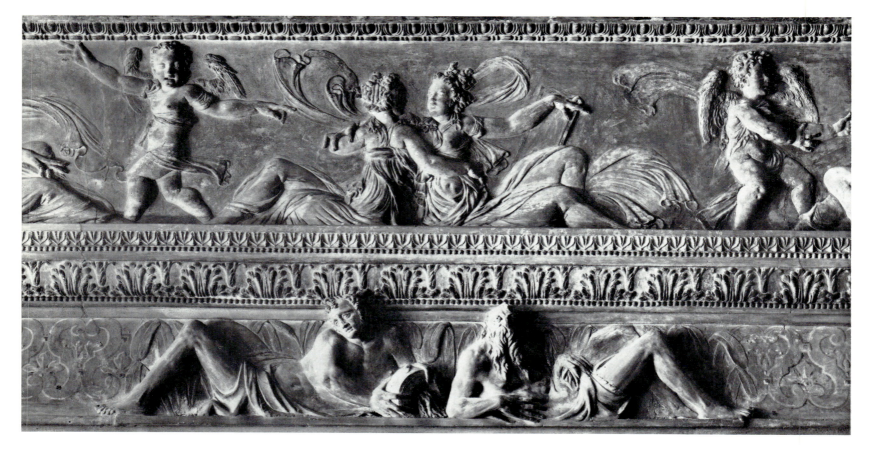

62 - Bartolomeo Ridolfi: stucco frieze in the study, detail

63 - Bartolomeo Ridolfi: stucco frieze in the study, detail

64 - Bartolomeo Ridolfi: stucco frieze in the study, detail

65 - Bartolomeo Ridolfi: stucco frieze in the study, detail

66 - BARTOLOMEO RIDOLFI: stucco frieze in the study, detail

67 - BARTOLOMEO RIDOLFI: stucco frieze in the study, detail

68 - BARTOLOMEO RIDOLFI: stucco frieze in the study, detail

69 - BARTOLOMEO RIDOLFI: stucco frieze in the study, detail

70 - GIAMBATTISTA TIEPOLO: bozzetto for the ceiling of the ground-floor salon. Seattle Art Museum

71 - GIAMBATTISTA TIEPOLO: fresco formerly on the ceiling of the ground-floor salon. Seattle Art Museum

72 - Giambattista Tiepolo: remnant of the detached fresco on the ceiling of the ground-floor salon

73 - GIAMBATTISTA TIEPOLO: remnant of the detached fresco on the ceiling of the ground floor salon, detail

74

75

76

77

78

79

74 - Giandomenico Tiepolo: *Francesco da Porto Named General of the Venetian Republic*
75 - Giandomenico Tiepolo: *Donato da Porto Made a Patrician of Venice*
76 - Giandomenico Tiepolo: *Ippolito da Porto Decorated by Charles V*
77 - Giandomenico Tiepolo: *Gerolamo da Porto Named Prefect of Piedmont*
78 - Giandomenico Tiepolo: *Giovanni Battista da Porto Named Commander-in-Chief*
79 - Giandomenico Tiepolo: *Jacopo da Porto Named Governor of Vicenza*

80-81-82-83 - Palazzo da Porto Festa: frescoes in the hallway between the room of the Giants and the ground-floor salon

84 - Palazzo da Porto Festa: cupola in the southeast corner room of the *piano nobile* with Pompeian motifs; a nine-teenth-century fresco

85 - Palazzo da Porto Festa: the Neoclassical rotunda on the *piano nobile*

86 - Palazzo da Porto Festa: cupola of the Neoclassical rotunda on the *piano nobile*

87 - Palazzo da Porto Festa: Neoclassical frieze in the rotunda on the *piano nobile*, detail of Homage to Architecture

88 -   Palazzo da Porto Festa: Neoclassical frieze in the rotunda on the *piano nobile*, detail of Homage to Sculpture

SCALE DRAWINGS

THE ARCHITECTURAL DRAWINGS WERE MADE BY PROF. ARCH. MARIO ZOCCONI AND BY DOTT. ARCH. ANDRZEJ PERESWIET-SOŁTAN, WITH THE ASSISTANCE OF DOTT. ARCH. EWA BORKOWSKA

89 - Palazzo da Porto Festa: Neoclassical frieze in the rotunda on the *piano nobile*, detail of probable portraits of Orazio Colleoni-Porto and Caterina Roncalli

90 - Palazzo da Porto Festa: Neoclassical frieze in the rotunda on the *piano nobile*, detail of Homage to Painting

0 5 10   50m

I - Palazzo da Porto Festa: topographical plan of the area

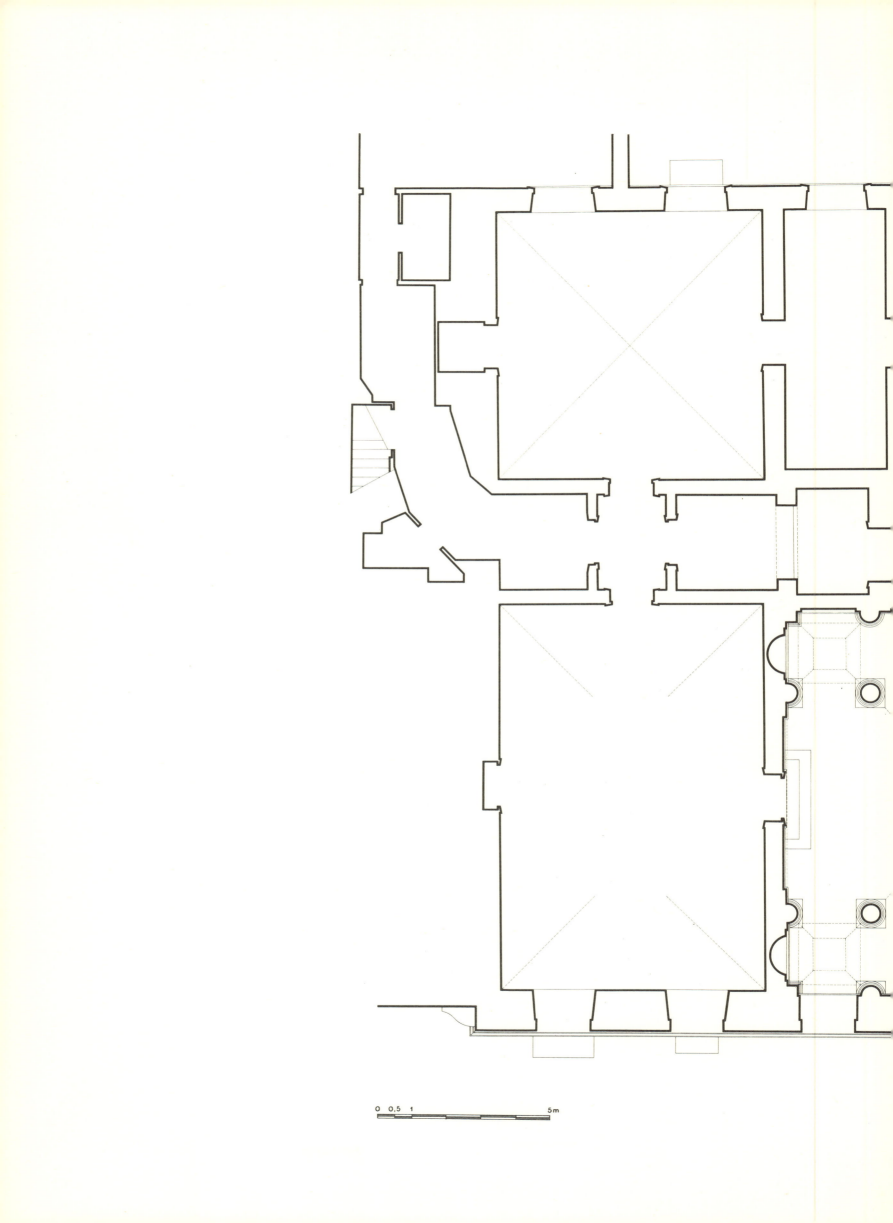

0 0,5 1   5m

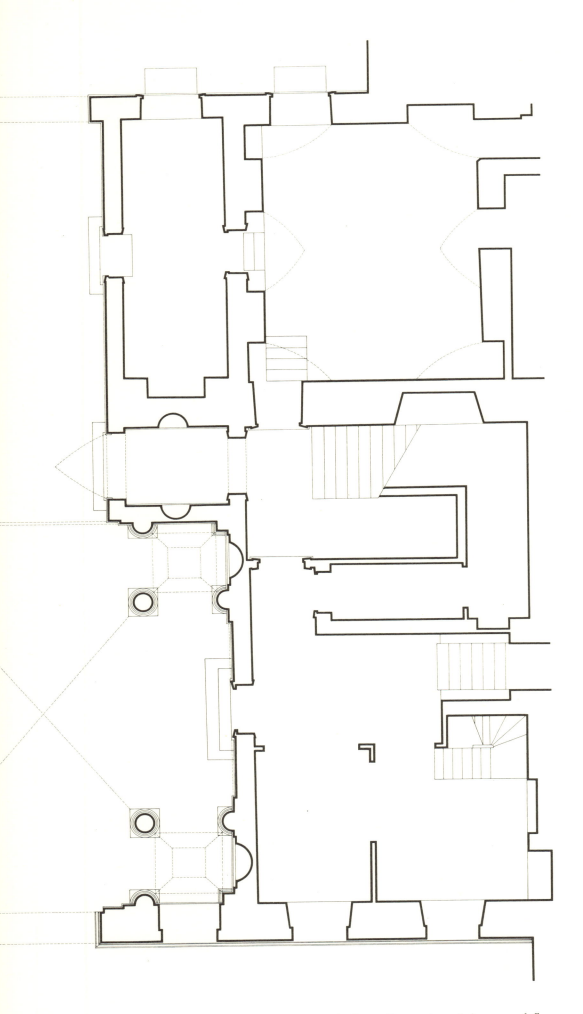

II - Palazzo da Porto Festa: plan of the ground floor

0 0,5 1   5m

III - Palazzo da Porto Festa: plan of the *piano nobile*

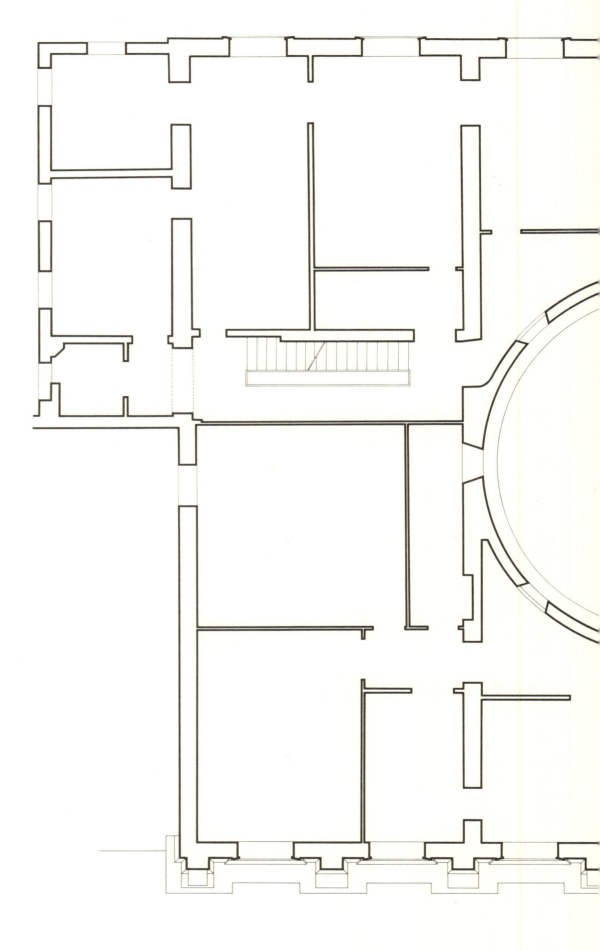

0 0,5 1   5m

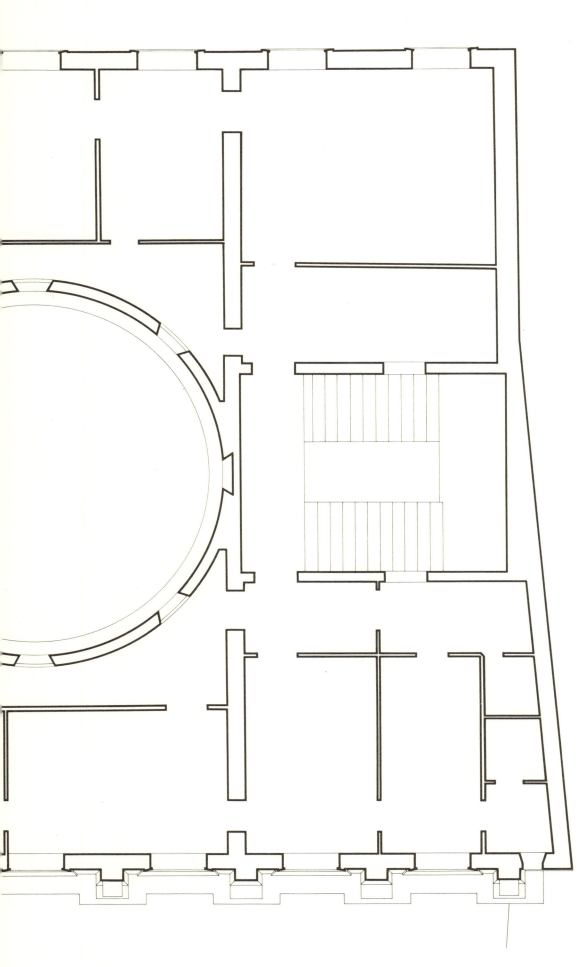

IV - Palazzo da Porto Festa: plan of the attic story

0 0,5 1   5m

CAHNERS *business information*

17273 SEVENTH STREET EAST, SONOMA, CA 95476

phone **707.939.9357** *fax* **707.939.9357** *e-mail* sonomastan@aol.com

STAN ABERCROMBIE | *books editor*

INTERIOR DESIGN® *magazine*

V - Palazzo da Porto Festa: elevation facing the street

0 0,5 1   5m

VI - Palazzo da Porto Festa: elevation facing the court

0 0,5 1   5m

VII - Palazzo da Porto Festa: longitudinal section, taken along the central axis